Eduardo

Pai An Workshop, Las Delicias, Peru

el Curandero:

The Words of a
Peruvian Healer

Eduardo Calderón
Richard Cowan
Douglas Sharon
F. Kaye Sharon

North Atlantic Books, Richmond, California

More people than we can note both in Peru and the United States have helped us with our work. With reference to this volume, however, we would especially like to thank Diana Muirhead for her assistance with the Spanish texts and Claire Schoenfeld and Fine Line Films for their aid with the photographs, while Paula Morrison has advised on all aspects of production. Beyond them, Richard Grossinger of North Atlantic Books has provided unflagging encouragement from his initial suggestion to do the book until its eventual conclusion, and Kathy Collins has been her usual helpful self. Thank you to everyone, named or merely remembered.

Published by North Atlantic Books
635 Amador Street
Richmond, California, 94805

Cover and Design by Paula Morrison

Typeset in Clarendon by Joe Safdie

Custom black and white photographic processing by Acu-Lab, San Francisco, Ca.

ISBN o-913028-95-9 paperback
ISBN 0-913028-94-0 cloth

Eduardo el Curandero is sponsored by the Society for the Study of Native Arts and Sciences, a nonprofit educational corporation whose goals are to develop an ecological and crosscultural perspective linking various scientific, social, and artistic fields; to nurture a holistic view of arts, sciences, humanities, and healing; and to publish and distribute literature on the relationship of mind, body, and nature.

TABLE OF CONTENTS

PREFACE

Eduardo Calderón is a Peruvian artist, fisherman, and healer *(curandero)* with a remarkable gift for alleviating disorders of the human psyche. This exceptional individual was the subject of our anthropological film, *Eduardo the Healer,* made in 1978. In this film we documented a day in Eduardo's life, showing him in a series of convivial interactions with his family and friends, talking to his assistants about his life and training as a *curandero* and conversing at the market place with *doña* Laura Sialer, an herbalist who once cured him of a love spell and introduced him to the world of the *curandero.* Paramount among the *curandero's* herbal remedies is the hallucinogenic San Pedro cactus, which has been in continuous use in Peruvian shamanism for over 3,000 years. As Eduardo indicates, *curanderos* use San Pedro to "see" directly into patients' ailments and to remove the cause of illness.

Eduardo the Healer depicted not only the customs of a *curandero,* but also the philosophy and beliefs of an articulate and perceptive man. Eduardo emerged as an immensely wise and gifted teacher whose abilities to divine and cure help his patients to achieve an improved self-image and a better understanding of the purpose of their lives. Now in *Eduardo el Curandero* we hope to augment his teachings by expanding what Eduardo said in the film and also by presenting valuable additional material which was beyond the scope of our original project.

Both book and film culminate in an all-night curing ceremony in which Eduardo uses the San Pedro cactus in concert with an elaborate blend of Indian and Christian rituals performed over a collection (or *mesa*) of shamanic power objects. As a result of his therapy, the village baker, Luciano Asmat, is released from a bad luck hex. David Harris, writing in the *Boston Phoenix,* describes this scene:

> The final section of the film, shot at night with the pounding sea in the background, is the powerful document of Eduardo's cure of a baker haunted by severe depression and inexplicable occurrences. Gradually, the man seems to emerge from the invisible grip of his mental chains.

Funded by the National Institute on Drug Abuse, one goal of the film was to demonstrate the important role that culture plays in the use of drugs. As the American anthropologist Peter Furst (1976:17) has stated:

> It is clearly society, not chemistry, that is the variable, since the same or chemically similar drugs can function so differently in different cultural situations, or be venerated over centuries as sacred, benign, and culturally integrative in some contexts but regarded in others as inherently so evil and dangerous that their very possession constitutes a serious crime.

What this means to us is that besides his intelligence, the single most important ingredient in Eduardo's healing is his profound humanity and charismatic personality. We know from personal experience that this is the key to his success with his patients, and suspect that such is the case with shamans in general.

Our efforts to produce an intimate portrait of Eduardo were greatly enhanced by the fact that all members of our team had a personal relationship with him. Douglas Sharon, who has spearheaded all work with Eduardo, has known him since 1965, and began research involving an apprenticeship with him in 1970. F. Kaye Sharon met the healer in 1974, and has been involved in her husband's work with Eduardo since its inception. As the ethnographic consultant for *Eduardo the Healer,* she transcribed and sensitively translated all texts for the film, which were ultimately selected and adapted by Richard Cowan for this book. Richard Cowan first worked with Eduardo in 1975 when he was directing a film on Moche art, *Discovering the Moche,* produced by Christopher Donnan, the archaeological consultant for *Eduardo the Healer.* In fact, the idea for a film on Eduardo was born during the filming of *Discovering the Moche,* since Eduardo's *mesa* and his curing rituals were used to explain the continuity of Moche shamanism from pre-Columbian times to the present. In the course of filming him, it became apparent how natural and spontaneous he was before the camera: his shamanism already had intrinsic appeal, but his personable presence was the deciding factor. A film about this man simply had to be made. Because Douglas Sharon was ethnographic consultant for *Discovering the Moche,* he, Richard Cowan, and Eduardo sat down in Peru and began planning for such a film.

Two years after *Discovering the Moche,* we found ourselves back in Peru filming Eduardo. Our cinematographer, Robert Primes, had no previous experience with anthropological films, but was a polished professional, and although there are numerous differences in philosophy and method between the anthropological and artistic approaches to filmmaking, we feel it safe to say that a synthesis of the two was achieved in *Eduardo the Healer.* Once the camera was rolling, it was apparent to all present that a silent and sympathetic dialogue between Robert Primes and Eduardo Calderón was occurring which clearly transcended the barriers

7

of language and culture. The rapport achieved between these two artists is what most anthropologists strive for with their informants, but very few attain. It is from Primes' footage that Richard Cowan and Paula Morrison selected the illustrations for this book.

Beyond our working relationship with Eduardo, while shooting the film we all became involved in his family life. The Sharons had previously established ritual kinship ties with him by becoming his *compadres* several years prior to the film, and before shooting was over so had the rest of the team. Not only did this increase our already close relationship with Eduardo and his family, but it gave us greater insight into his shamanism and the way in which it influences his daily life. For example, we observed an incident which clearly illustrates the interaction between Eduardo's roles as healer and father. When we arrived in Peru in February, 1977, Eduardo's third youngest son, Paco, was limping badly, and we were told that although the injury had resulted from a fall from an adobe wall, the accident was caused by witchcraft. It turned out that a neighbor had been keeping pigs, a business prohibited by law, and the flies from them were affecting Eduardo's well and recently inaugurated restaurant. Eduardo had notified the authorities, who removed the pigs, and in retaliation, the neighbor hired a sorcerer to work a spell on Eduardo, who had proved too strong to succumb. The spell had not taken effect, so the sorcerer had focused successfully on Paco.

Prior to our arrival, Eduardo had diagnosed the injury and performed a curing ritual for his son. This session had partially removed the hex, aiding the efforts of his physician, a bone specialist whose therapy up to that point had proved unsuccessful, and incidentally providing an example of the way in which many contemporary healers view their therapy as complementary to modern medicine. Two more sessions were required for Paco, and we were all in agreement that they would provide excellent material for the film

The rituals performed for Paco were very touching. They occurred at about 2 a.m. and it was cold, but seven-year-old Paco was awakened, gently nudged out of his warm blankets, and sent to stand in front of the *mesa*. There he stood, shivering and rubbing his sleep-laded eyelids. On one occasion his oldest sister, Julia, even rushed out and buttoned his sweater to help him keep warm. Meanwhile, his father did a *florecimiento* ("flowering") ritual—rubbing him with an herb jar, having him nasally imbibe some herbal liquid, and then spraying him with the potion. Eduardo performed this ritual with the same brisk flare and confidence he applied to all his patients. His ministrations were firm but gentle, he knew exactly what he was doing, and Paco responded quietly and respectfully. Hardly a word was exchanged, and when it was over, Paco dived into the comfort of the blankets extended to him by his mother and sister.

One of the tragedies of our film is that this priceless scene could not be used, since technical problems resulted in grainy footage for many of the

8

night episodes. Fortunately, however, our film editor, Lee Rhoads, was able to piece together the usable portions into a coherent entity. His extraordinary sensitivity to Eduardo's cultural background, idiosyncracies, and linguistic nuances—together with a most exemplary dedication to the thematic unity of his subject matter—resulted in a product for which all participants owe him a very special note of thanks.

The socio-economic conditions underlying Paco's case are typical of most cases of witchcraft. Ultimately, they can be traced back to disturbed social relationships, which are often triggered by an economic issue in an emerging nation. The witchcraft syndrome thus serves as an "escape valve," permitting hostility to be expressed without disrupting fundamental social institutions. Eduardo's neighbor could not do anything about the law against pigs; however, by seeking the services of a sorcerer, he could at least find an outlet for his pent-up aggression.

Luciano Asmat's misfortunes demonstrate another way in which social conditions perpetuate witchcraft. In his case, the witchcraft was a vehicle for "institutionalized envy," a mechanism by which the status quo is supported in a poor community by an individual being discouraged from improving his socio-economic status. In northern Peru, a rigid social system combines with limited economic opportunities and high unemployment to create a situation where the successful entrepreneur can often be perceived as a threat to the community as a whole. Thus, a person who substantially improves his standard of living may become the target of gossip, ostracism, and witchcraft.

Prior to his streak of bad luck, Luciano's bakery had been prospering. He had bought a car, which he was using as a taxi, and things were going very well—indeed, too well. People began to talk. Why was this formerly poor baker so successful? People stopped buying his bread, his profits dwindled away, his debts began to accrue, and he was forced to sell his taxi. Family quarrels developed. His children had nightmares and did poorly in school. Things had gotten so bad that he had abandoned the family to look for a job in another town. He could not find work, however, and had decided to return and attempt to solve his financial problems. This is when he came to Eduardo. After three sessions, Eduardo had broken the spell, and Luciano had successfully resumed his business. The third session, a "flowering" or closure ritual, is the one seen in the film.

Thus we have two anthropological "explanations" for witchcraft. But is the healer's therapy successful? With regard to Paco and Luciano, we can state an unequivocal yes. The film team observed their therapy from beginning to end and witnessed complete remission of all symptoms; furthermore, Douglas Sharon was able to follow-up on the results in the course of subsequent visits to Peru. Paco's leg is completely healed and Luciano's fortunes have continued to improve steadily. In addition, case histories collected in 1979-80 by Douglas Sharon and Donald Skillman, a UCLA doctorate candidate in anthropology, have revealed that a majority of patients interviewed after treatment indicate complete satisfaction with *curandero* therapy, while the remainder indicate there has been definite improvement in their condition, but feel the need for an additional session with the healer. All patients were unanimous in declaring that therapy had greatly bolstered their self-image and restored their confidence to overcome the specific social and psychological circumstances of their particular problems.

What, then, is the dynamic underlying a "successful cure?" The answer to this problem leads us to what can best be referred to as the "dialectic of good versus evil" underlying Eduardo's therapy. This dualistic ideology is most apparent in the spatial arrangement of Eduardo's *mesa* and in the rituals performed over it. For example, the power objects on the *mesa* are always laid out in a pattern where "good" artifacts are placed on the right and "evil" are on the left, with a "middle field" or "mediating center" between them. Eduardo's rituals symbolically "charge" the *mesa*, i.e. activate a dialectical process by which the forces of good and evil are brought into meaningful interaction through the mediation of the middle field. The power of the harmony of opposites is symbolically "discharged" in a cure, i.e. transmitted to the patient to help him balance disharmonies in his body and psyche.

When we completed the film in 1978, we did not know how representative of north Peruvian shamanism Eduardo's ideology might be. However, in that year Douglas Sharon began expanding his network of shaman informants. At this writing, eight more shamans are cooperating with him, and from 1980-81 Don Joralemon, a doctoral candiate in anthropology from UCLA, has worked intensively with yet another healer. We now know beyond the shadow of a doubt that north Peruvian *mesas* and curing rituals are all remarkably similar in form and function; that all shamans to date share the same ideology of mediated dualism discovered in Eduardo's therapy. All, in fact, use variants of the same occult terminology employed by Eduardo.

With the foregoing theoretical framework in mind, we can now address how Eduardo's dialectic is applied in actual therapy. How are the balanced energies of good and evil accumulated by the charged *mesa* discharged or transmitted to the patient? Eduardo uses the term "magnetism" to explain this process. Here is his definition:

> Magnetic force is one of the innate essences in the individual . . . The magnetic current rises up the left leg and down the right . . . The mind corresponds to the electromagnetic field and acts as the general battery. The encephalic cavity is at the same time the accumulator and the generator of currents which govern these things . . . The ends of the fingers are the antennae from which the magnetic current emanates or sparks.

Magnetism is the activating electrical force of the individual to unite with others. All have a magnetic . . . force linked with the earth, since all are elements of the earth. Thus by forming a magnetic chain, the attraction of the individuals, the telepathic force, the intellectual effort unites all beings along this nexus . . . Magnetism is the thread and the telepathic force is the transmission . . . along the thread (Sharon 1978:51-2).

Eduardo's use of an electromagnetic analogy to explain how healing works differs only in its degree of sophistication from explanations given by other northern healers. Many compare the healing process to electricity without being able to fully explain what they mean, and, for the most part, they all agree that the interaction between good or positive energies and bad or negative energies is required to produce a balanced synthesis or concentration of "power," which must then be transmitted to patients in order to help them attain the same kind of reconciliation of forces within their own bodies and minds.

This reconciliation of opposites operative in north Peruvian shamanism shows a striking similarity to the balancing of *yin* and *yang* in Chinese medicine and philosophy. It is also reminiscent of recent work concerned with the different functions of the left and right hemispheres of the human brain. In fact, the concept of the union of contraries recurs time and time again in the myths, rituals, beliefs, symbols, and mystical techniques of cultures everywhere. In effect, northern shamans are attempting to "translate" a core belief of universal archaic shamanism into modern terminology. When stripped of all its mythopoetic imagery, this principle is the pantheistic or animatistic idea of "power," which contends that underlying all the visible forms of the world is a mysterious, impersonal essence from which they emerge and by which they are sustained until they are inevitably reabsorbed. Although this power is everywhere, it tends to be focused in sacred objects, plants, and places. Everyone commands some vestige of power, but it is only the shaman who is in direct contact with it in accord with his or her inner nature. The shaman's personal power is revealed in charisma, ritual knowledge, and wisdom about the true nature of things. Its most graphic applications are in artistic expression and curing.

There is a great deal that the growing field of transcultural psychiatry[1] can learn from the shaman, as the world-renowned Peruvian social psychiatrist, Carlos Alberto Seguin (1970:159) has pointed out in address-

[1]For discussions of the scope of cultural, transcultural, or ethnopsychiatry see Kiev 1972, Kennedy 1974, and Foster and Anderson (1978:81-100).

ing the First National Congress of Peruvian Psychiatry in Lima in October, 1969. At this meeting, Seguin referred to *curanderos* as "colleagues," and he praised them for knowledge of hallucinogens and group dynamics—areas that psychiatry was just then "discovering." In a similar vein, the American ethnopsychiatrist E. Fuller Torrey (1972:1) has delineated the implications of recognizing traditional practitioners as psychotherapeutic allies: "It suggests new sources of mental health manpower... (and) radically different types of mental health services for other countries." Likewise, another American ethnopsychiatrist, Ari Kiev (1972:182-6), has recommended the utilization of native healers in the psychiatric programs of developing countries, indicating that:

> The value of native healers lies in their knowledge of the members of the community and of the culture ... The modern psychiatrist can learn from the native healer, whose beliefs and practices have not developed willy-nilly, but in response to specific problems of the members of the culture.

The Barefoot Doctor program in China was an initial attempt to combine ancient and modern approaches to healing, and another effort of this kind was instituted by the Nigerian psychiatrist, Dr. Thomas A. Lambo, who included traditional practitioners on the staff of a hospital located in Yoruba country. Besides gaining the confidence of rural patients, Dr. Lambo's program also trained native healers in some of the basic principles of Western psychiatry, as well as exposed Western-trained psychiatrists to folk healing (Lambo 1964).[2] Dr. Lambo is now Deputy Director-General of the United Nations World Health Organization (WHO) at Geneva, where in 1975 he began an initiative to encourage the integration of traditional therapists into public health programs in developing nations (Singer 1977:242-52). This initiative led to the formation of a WHO Working Group on Traditional Medicine headed by Dr. R. H. Bannerman who conducted a two year study of traditional curing.

Dr. Bannerman's results, which were reported to the executive board of WHO, contended: 1) that most traditional healers are thoroughly trained, 2) that in developing countries they constitute the major health resource for nine-tenths of the rural population, and 3) that they are usually consulted in preference to other health workers. His study recommended that interdisciplinary investigations into the psychosocial and anthropological aspects of traditional medicine soon be conducted (*To The Point* 5:30, May 26, 1978). WHO's position on traditional therapy is presented in its Technical Report Series, No. 622, "The Promotion and Devel-

---

[2]A review of the success of Lambo's program, twenty years later, is provided in the documentary film, *Nigerian Doctors.*

opment of Traditional Medicine." On page 13, the rationale for this position is given, stating that traditional medicine:

> . . . is already the people's own health care system and is well accepted by them. It has certain advantages over imported systems of medicine in any setting because, as an integral part of the people's culture, it is particularly effective in solving certain cultural health problems. It can and does freely contribute to scientific and universal medicine.

In the Western Hemisphere, WHO's Regional Office for the Americas, the Pan American Health Organization (PAHO) has been attempting to follow Geneva's initiative. One result of this effort has been Scientific Publication No. 359, released in 1978 in Washington, D.C., which reports on a workshop on "Modern Medicine and Medical Anthropology in the United States-Mexico Border Population." Regarding a course of action for the Americas, one important recommendation made by the participants suggested that PAHO:

> support training programs for a variety of traditional healers, keeping in mind that they must be allowed to maintain their authority and position within the community rather than being disenfranchised by incorporation into the official health system (p. 210).

In Peru, Seguin (1977) has advocated an approach similar to that of WHO and PAHO in calling for an in-depth, interdisciplinary study of traditional medicine with the ultimate aims of discovering new applications of folk therapy to modern medicine and of incorporating the *curandero* into the modern institutional framework. Seguin proposes two methods for achieving these goals: 1) the establishment of a Department of Folkloric Medicine in each School of Medicine in Peru, and 2) the organization of systematic research on traditional medicine to be undertaken by graduating medical students. By these means, he hopes to achieve a collaboration between traditional and modern medicine as a pragmatic and efficient way to overcome the current lack of medical personnel in rural areas where: "the young doctor . . . finds that all his knowledge has no value, that his techniques cannot be employed, and that the town *curandero* is capable and knows more than he does" (1974:328).

A first step toward implementing Seguin's suggestions has been made at the School of Medicine of the National University of Trujillo. Here, in August, 1978 and again in October, 1979, Douglas Sharon taught a course on folk healing, the first ever given in Peru, using the Spanish version of *Eduardo the Healer*, as well as a book in Spanish, *Terapia de la curanderia,*

13

co-authored especially for the course by Sharon and Eduardo Calderón with a grant from the Tinker Foundation, New York. Eduardo also taught a segment of the course dealing with his *mesa*, folk diagnosis, and the use of herbs.

This course was meant to prepare advanced medical students for their one year of obligatory social service in underserved areas of the country, a pre-requisite to graduation under innovative Peruvian public health programs instituted in the mid 1970's. Its goal was to demonstrate how folk medicine perpetuates itself at the grassroots level through oral tradition, imitative learning, and a socio-economic network supported by traditional beliefs and practices, and to help sensitize young doctors to traditional medical lore. Hopefully, this will improve communication between practitioners of old and new techniques, and will permit modern health workers to use local networks and human resources to channel medical innovations. Eventually, an environment may be created that will foster a mutual exchange of concepts and practices between traditional and modern therapy.

To bring the collaborative message home, it is becoming increasingly apparent that even in the United States cooperation between traditional and modern psychotherapy can make a valuable contribution to the promotion of better mental health, particularly among ethnic minorities. For example, at the Lincoln Community Health Center in the Bronx, New York, Pedro Ruiz, a psychiatrist, and John Langrod, a psychologist (1976a, 1976b, 1976c, 1977), have been very successful in combining traditional and modern methods to meet the psychiatric needs of the predominantly Puerto Rican community served by this center. Therapy here has thus included the use of folk healers, and residents in psychiatry have additionally been exposed to the methods of folk medicine through an in-service training program. Extensive research has also been conducted into such folk practices as *espiritismo* (spiritualism), which—interestingly enough—uses *mesas* in its therapy (Harwood 1977).

In California, on November 16, 1981 the *Los Angeles Times* published a lengthy report on the persistence of Mexican folk medicine in local *barrios,* noting how some Latino medical personnel are attempting to blend the old with the modern. For example, Dr. Arnoldo Solis, a psychiatrist at Martin Luther King, Jr. Hospital in South-Central Los Angeles, tells of how he began to combine orthodox and folk medicine after he discovered that the strictly orthodox approach was ineffective with many of his Latino patients. For instance, Dr. Solis might instruct a patient to take his anti-psychotic medication ritualistically in an herb tea, and he might also prescribe a spiritual cleansing. Similarly, Dr. Henry Herrera, director of the psychiatric consultation liaison service at the University of California, Davis, School of Medicine is testing the importance of folk medicine in an effort to explain data showing that Mexican-Americans underutilize health facilities. After observing a Mexican folk healer, Dr.

Herrera has reported that he was "overwhelmingly impressed with the healer's incredible, natural empathy toward the patient . . . the healer's ability to draw out painful but key episodes in a patient's life . . . using the skills that the best psychotherapist might use."

Returning to the subject of our film and book, the ubiquitous Eduardo is now right in the middle of this dialogue. In May and June of 1981, he was the guest of Douglas Sharon at the San Diego Museum of Man, coming to San Diego as a visiting scholar to participate in a Latin American-style *clausura* (closing) for the Museum's "Flight of the Jaguar" exhibit, which dealt with South American shamanism. Part of the show featured a replica of Eduardo's *mesa* along with a life-size photograph of the shaman, and Eduardo's role in the *clausura* was literally to step out of a display case and make the exhibit live with a "hands-on" demonstration of the *mesa*. His two-hour presentation, which was video-taped, inaugurated a seminar series on South American shamanism which included the participation of leading international scholars.

Besides his Museum appearance and a press conference, Eduardo's ten day visit to California included talks at the Centro Cultural de la Raza, at the University of California, San Diego and at the University of California, Los Angeles; and he was also interviewed on a radio talk show, profiled in the local newspapers, and presented on television. Eduardo's warmth and outgoing manner won the hearts and minds of many San Diegans, in spite of the limitations of speaking through an interpretor. As usual, he was articulate, enthusiastic, and completely open. Total conviction that shamanism is meaningful and relevant in a world of increasing complexity pervaded his discourse. His visit was a living testimony to the importance of his tireless efforts in developing an ongoing dialogue between traditional and modern medicine.

Eduardo el Curandero
The Words of a Peruvian Healer

THE CALDERÓN FAMILY AT BREAKFAST

MARÍA: *¡Qué rica mermelada!*
What good marmalade!

EDUARDO: *Qué rica. ¿Quieres toyo?*
Yes, it is good. Do you want some fish?

MARÍA: *¡Amarga!*
It's bitter!

EDUARDO: *Oye. Vamos a tener una curación esta noche. Es*
Listen. We're going to have a cure tonight. It's

para un muchacho se llama Asmat. Tu sabes, el panadero de
for a guy named Asmat. You know, the baker at

Moche.
Moche.

MARÍA: *Sí, sí. Lo requerdo.*
Oh yeah. I remember him.

EDUARDO: *Bueno. Tú comprarás el maíz molido blanco, los*
Good. You go buy the white corn meal, the

flores, y las limas . . .
flowers, and the sweet limes . . .

MARÍA: *Ya, ya.*
OK.

EDUARDO: *Y yo voy a ir a comprarme las hierbas y los San*
And I'm going to buy the herbs and the San

Pedros a la señora Laura. ¡Siéntate Martín!
Pedros at Laura's stand. Sit down Martín!

MARTÍN: *¡Voy a comerme mi dulce!*
I'm going to eat my sweets!

MARÍA: *¡Malcriado es!*
He's being bad!

EDUARDO: *Van a venir como siete, ocho personas,*
About seven or eight people are going to come,

y a los alzadores, ahora hay que avisarle a mi compadre
and for assistants, you notify my *compadre*

Juan y don Alberto . . .
Juan and *don* Alberto . . .

MARTÍN: *¡Yo también voy a ir!*
I'm going too!

EDUARDO: *Y Martín de alzador.*
And Martín as assistant.

MARÍA: *Muy enano, muy enano.*
A very small one, very small.

EDUARDO: *Yo voy a ir a comprar tres San Pedros: buenos*
I'm going to buy three San Pedros: good ones

del norte para que verán los diablos. Necesitamos
from the north so they'll see the devils! We need

buenos para que media lata está
good ones so that half a can of "remedy" is

suficiente.
sufficient.

MARÍA: *Hay que hacerlo menos que no merma ya.*
We should make less, so it's not wasted.

EDUARDO: *Un vaso por cabeza tiene que ser.*
One glass per head, that's how it must be.

MARÍA: *Tres cuartos para Martín.*
Three quarters for Martín.

EDUARDO: *Medio vaso, no se le puede dar más. Y a*
Half a glass. We can't give him more. And for

las señoras que sepan embarazada,
those women who know that they're pregnant,

no se puede dar tampoco.
we can't give them any.

MARÍA: *¡Es peligroso!*
It's dangerous!

EDUARDO: *Necesitamos también la agua florida, y no te olvides mi*
We also need scented water, and don't forget my

chaleco, mi chaleco . . .
vest, my vest . . .

MARÍA: *¡Y tu gorro!*
And your beret!

EDUARDO: *Vamos.*
Let's go!

EDUARDO BUYING SAN PEDRO
AT DOÑA LAURA SIALER'S HERB STAND

EDUARDO: *¿Cómo está, doña Laura?*
            How are you, *doña* Laura?

LAURA: *¿Qué tal? ¿Cómo te has acordado de mí,*
            How goes it? How is it you've remembered me,

            la que te dió la vida?
            the one who gave you life?

EDUARDO: *Claro, yo me acuerdo de usted, pues, tía. A ver,*
            Of course I remember you, auntie. Let's see, I

            necesito unos San Pedritos.
            need some San Pedros . . .

LAURA: *Buenos del norte. Huaringueños.*
Good ones from the north, from the Huaringa

De esos que hagan zapatear, pues.
lagoons. The ones that make you kick.

EDUARDO: *¿Unos tres, ah? Y un poco de condor.*
Three, huh? And a little *condor* herb.

LAURA: *¿Condor misha o condor purga?*
Hallucinogenic *condor* or purgative *condor*?

EDUARDO: *Condor misha.*
Condor misha.

LAURA: *¿Qué otra cosa quiere usted?*
What else do you need?

EDUARDO: *Pasca, pasquita blanca. Está bien para el refresco*
Lime, white lime. It's good for "refreshment" at

al final de una sesión.
the end of a curing session.

LAURA: *¿Qué otra cosita?*
What else?

EDUARDO: *Bueno, ya con eso basta, suficiente. Aquí tía*
Well, with that it's enough, sufficient. I'm just

a visitarla. ¿Se acuerda usted cuando
here to visit you. Do you remember when you

me curó?
cured me?

LAURA: *¿Cómo no me voy a acordar? Por mí existe usted.*
How could I forget? Because of me you exist.

¿Es así o no?
Isn't that so?

EDUARDO: *Claro.*
Of course.

LAURA: *¿De qué edad?*
How old were you?

EDUARDO: *Diecisiete años, pues.*
Seventeen years old.

LAURA: *¿Por qué fué? ¿Por travieso? ¿Por el amor?*
What was it for? Mischief? Love?

EDUARDO: *¿Cómo estaba yo?*
How was I?

LAURA: *¡Estabas tú para el cementerio! Pero gracias*
You were ready for the cemetery! But thanks to

a doña Laura, que te dió a ti la vida . . .
me, *doña* Laura, who gave you back your life . . .

EDUARDO: *Pura yerba, pura yerba. Sí me acuerdo que me hizo sacar*
Pure herbs, pure herbs. I remember you turned

el estómago y a volverlo a meter
my stomach inside out and put it back in again

para rasquetearlo.
in order to scrub it.

23

LAURA: *¡Te dí un purgante que te hizo arrojar la tierra!*
I gave you a purge that made you throw up dirt!

Ya, tu mama decía, "¡Ay, mi hijo se muere!"
Yes, your mother said, "Ay, my son is dying!"

—No se muere, le dije, tiembla, tiembla.
"He isn't dying," I said. "He's trembling."

—¡Ay no, mi hijo se muere!
"No, my son is dying!"

—No se muere. Déjelo, que tiene que
"He's not dying, leave him alone. He has to

botar todo que le han dado a él por
throw up everything they gave him for being a

cervecero, limeño, y enamorador.
beer guzzler, a city slicker, and a wencher."

¡Por una muchacha! Venir de Lima donde
Hexed because of a girl! You came from Lima

los mejores médicos te habían visto, no te
where the best doctors had seen you, and not

hacían ninguna. Pero yo con mis pequeñeces,
one did anything for you. But me with my little

mis yerbitas, lo sané al caballero, gordo
things, my herbs, I made the gentleman well, fat

y lleno de vida. Listo para la profesión. Ahora
and full of life. Ready for the profession. Now

tú eres mi maestro mió.
you are my teacher.

EDUARDO: *No, ya no es así. Sigue siendo la catedrática.*
No, that's not so. You are still the professor.

LAURA: *Todo lo contrario. Ahora tú eres mi maestro.*
On the contrary. Now you are my teacher.

EDUARDO TELLS ABOUT HIS LIFE

Yo soy de Trujillo. Todos creen que soy mochero, pero soy
I'm from Trujillo. Everyone thinks I'm from Moche, but I'm

trujillano. De la portada de Moche. Yo nací el año treinta.
from Trujillo. From the part nearest to Moche. I was born in

El cuatro de junio, un día viernes a las cuatro de la mañana.
1930. The fourth of June, a Friday at four in the morning.

Mi mamá, mi papá me criaron. Mi mamá me quería mucho.
My mother and father raised me. My mother loved me a lot.

Mi papá era un artesano, un zapatero, buen zapatero. Desde
My father was an artisan, a shoemaker, a good shoemaker. I've

muchacho he trabajado yo. Después del colegio, traía comida para los cuyes,
worked since I was a boy. After school, I used to feed the guinea

los conejos. Comimos conejo, pues. ¡Harto conejo! Mi mamá
pigs and rabbits. We ate rabbit then. Lots of rabbit! My mother

25

hizo un esfuerzo y pobremente, y yo trabajando, por supuesto, también,
worked hard and earned little, and, of course, I had to work too,

siempre moviendo la mano para abrigarse. Así terminé la primaria,
always struggling to help support us. I finished grade school

trabajando.
that way, working.

La familia por la parte de mi padre son serranos. Mi madre
The family on my father's side are highlanders. My mother,

también. Cajabambinos. ¡Ahí saben estudiar! Mi
too. From Cajabamba. They know how to study there! My

abuelo, mis tios, mi papá, todos en el seminario,
grandfather, my uncles, and my father all went to the seminary

y me pusieron al Seminario el año 1947. Toda mi familia
high school, and they put me in the Seminary in 1947. All my

pertenece a la línea de eclesiasticos por parte de mi tatarabuelo.
family belongs to the ecclesiastical line from my great grand-

Yo tengo mis tios curas, y por supuesto, yo tuve también la inclinación
father on. I have uncles who are priests, and, of course, I wanted

ser cura, pues.
to be a priest too.

Mucho me gustaba ser sacerdote. Estudié dos
I liked the idea of being a priest very much. I studied two

años. Usé sotana. Pero, después me desanimé.
years. I wore a cassock. But after awhile I became discouraged.

Estaba bién bravo. Más bién que ser mal cura, dije, "Mejor
It was very tough. Rather than be a bad priest, I said, "It's better

estoy así, tranquilo." Aquí hago los bautizos, agua del socorro,
to be here, tranquil." Here I perform baptisms, rites for the sick,

agua del bién morir. A bendecir una cosa. En fin, tanta cosita. Todo es
rites for the dead. I bless things. In short, little tasks. All this

por inclinación de familia. Terminé el seminario el año
because of the family inclination. I finished the seminary in

'50, '51.
'50, '51.

Yo quise ser médico, pero no se pude en aquél entonces.
I wanted to be a doctor, but that wasn't possible in those

Para ser médico había que tener plata, pues. Un libro costaba un
days. To be a doctor then, one had to have money. A book cost a

montón de plata, y yo que ganaba apenas.
pile of money, and I earned little.

Total, que como yo destaqué en la cuestión del arte, el arte digamos
The end result was that since I had a talent for art, that is to

de la escultura, me decidí a irme. Mi mamá, mis tios, mi
say sculpture, I decided to leave. My mother, my uncles, my

familia me dijeron, "¿Qué vas a aprender a hacer
family all said, "Are you really going to learn how to make

muñecos? No vas a vivir de eso. Eso no
dolls? You're not going to be able to live off that. There's no

es plata."
money in that."

De todas maneras, yo me mandé mudar. Entonces, junté mi plata y me fuí
In any case, I left. I got together my money and I went to

a Lima, a la Escuela de Bellas Artes. Ingresé el año '50, '51. Mi
Lima, to the School of Fine Arts. I entered in '50, '51. My great

anhelo fué de ser escultor. Yo siempre había leído y
desire was to be a sculptor. I always read a great deal and

hacía mis dibujos, pero desgraciadamente no era como yo
practiced my drawings, but unfortunately it was not the way I

pensaba, la Escuela de Bellas Artes. La Escuela de Bellas
thought the School of Fine Arts would be. The School of Fine

Artes piensa que está para hacer artistas, pero es mentira. El
Arts thinks that it is there to make artists, but that's a lie. The

artista nace, no sale. Desde que nace tiene
artist is born, not made. From the moment he is born he has

talento latente. La escuela puede templar el caráctar, pero como una
latent talent. School can help to temper character, but as a

fábrica de artistas, es un engaño.
factory for artists, it's a deception.

Me salí al año, no más, y comencé a trabajar
I left that place within the first year and began to work

solo. Compraba mi barro yo por arrobas y comenzaba a hacer mis
alone. I bought my clay by the pound and began to make my

dibujos. La mejor escuela que he tenido ha sido los mochicas,
figures. The best school that I have had has been the Mochicas,

los huacos mochicas. Yo paraba metido en el
the ancient Mochica ceramics. I used to spend hours in the

Museo Nacional de Antropología. Ahí el día domingo con mi bolsa
National Museum of Anthropology. Every Sunday with my bag

de dulces, de pan, y de fruta. El primero en entrar y el último en salir.
of sweets, bread, and fruit. I was the first in and the last to leave.

Me tenían que botar, con mi cuaderno, mis libros. Dibujando
They had to throw me out, with my copy book, my books. Draw-

un huaco por todos sus lados y modelándolo en mi casa, eso fué
ing ceramics from all sides and modeling in my house, that was

mi mejor maestro.
my best teacher.

Yo estudiaba de noche y trabajaba de día de ayudante
I studied at night and worked by day as a bricklayer's

de abañil. Ganaba una miséria en Lima. Hacía frío.
assistant. I earned a miserable sum in Lima. It was cold. I was

Mal comido. Pero yo me las ingeniaba. Me iba los dias sábados al
poorly fed. But I managed. Every Saturday I went to the fisher-

muelle de pescadores a Agua Dulce a sacar cangrejos, a agarrar patillos.
man's wharf at Agua Dulce to fish for crabs and catch sea gulls.

A sacarlos ahí para comer, pues.
I used to catch them in order to eat.

Así estaba, pues. No había fichas casi, entonces agarré
That's the way it was. I was almost out of money, so I packed

y me vine para acá y pensé meterme a pescar. Entonces me
up and came back home and decided to try fishing. I found

29

encontré con mi tío Arcario, y me dijo, "¿Quieres
myself with my Uncle Arcario then, and he said to me, "Do you

ir a pescar, hijo?" "Ya pues," pero en ese tiempo no sabía
want to fish, son?" "Sure," but in those days I didn't know a

de pescar. Ni chango, ni chanos.
thing about fishing. Not even in jest.

Me acuerdo la primera vez que gané, la primera pesca que hice y
I remember the first time I earned, the first time I fished and

que me dió mi plata. Fuí y se los dí a mi mamá. Entonces, mi
earned good money. I went and gave it to my mother. Then, my

mamá se enorgulló, pero dijo, "¿Vas a seguir
mother was proud of me, but she said, "Are you going to con-

de pescador?" Bueno, me gustó la pesca, pues. Estaba en todas
tinue as a fisherman?" Well, I liked fishing. I was in the prime of

mis años. Veintiún años.
youth. Twenty-one years old.

Bueno, comencé. Me traje acá a Las Delicias y comenzamos a pescar muy
Well, I started. I came here to Las Delicias and began to fish

bién. Hemos ido a pescar con mi chinchorro de cuatro. ¡Unas corvinazas enormes!
well. We used to fish with my four man net. Huge bass! They

Tiraba mi brazo. Me conocí a María en aquel entonces. Tuvimos el
stretched out my arms. I met Maria at that time. We had our first

primer hijo, Chochi.
son, Chochi.

Entonces, nos hemos ido a Chimbote, y en Chimbote comencé a trabajar
Then we went to Chimbote, and in Chimbote I began to work

en las anchoveteras para un harinero de pescado. Gané plata, pero
the schools of anchovy for a fish meal company. I made money,

nos teníamos que romper el alma en el mar. Después de un tiempo, nos hemos
but we had to work our tails off at sea. After a while, we returned

venido nuevamente, y me compré un chinchorro nuevecitito que yo mismo armé
here again, and I bought a new net, which I myself put together

acá, con un bote. ¡Cómo se ganaba, y en un ratito! Me
here, with a boat. How we made money, and in a short time! I

decidí seguir trabajando en la pesca, pero como yo había estudiado la cuestión
decided to continue fishing, but since I had studied the business

del arte, me dediqué también ya a hacer trabajos de escultura.
of art, I also dedicated myself to doing works of sculpture.

Tuve más hijos más allá, y me abrí, pero entonces pasé
I had more children later on, and I continued to advance, but

un tiempo malo. No había pesca, y comencé a trabajar en
times went bad. There were no fish, and I started to work in the

la cuestión del arte. ¡Dale que dale! Las primeras piezas se las vendí al Dr.
art business. Giving it all I had! I sold the first pieces to Dr.

Miranda, cuando estaba yo un poco mal de los pies. Hacía mis
Miranda when I had a little trouble with my feet. I made wood

obras de madera, y me pagaba un precio a ese tiempo.
carvings, and he paid me the going price for those times.

¡Cuando llegó el Hope en el año 1962, comencé a vender!
When the Project Hope ship arrived in 1962, I began to sell!

Como me veían mis obras de escultura de madera, de cerámica, entonces
As they saw my works in wood sculpture and ceramics, they

se interesaron y comenzaron a comprar cantidad de cosas. Yo comencé
became interested, and began to buy a great many. I began to

a tener plata ya, con eso de las esculturas. Me ofrecieron
have money again from the sale of my sculptures. They even

un contrato de cinco años para irme a los Estados Unidos, pero me
offered me a five year contract to go to the United States, but I

quedé acá porque mi mamá estaba enferma.
stayed here because my mother was sick.

Entonces me llamó Chan Chan; en la restauración me hizo un trabajo.
Then I was called to work on the restoration of Chan Chan.

Un pedido de que me acercara a ver si tomara a cargo
A request came for me to come over and see if I wanted to take

la línea de restauración de las ruinas de Tschudi.
charge of the restoration of the ancient ruins of the Tschudi

Como ya más o menos conocía yo de esta cuestión, entré yo,
complex. As I more or less knew that kind of work, I took over,

¿y para que? Allí he trabajado seis años.
and why not? I worked there six years.

Me acuerdo también cuando yo tenía diecisiete años, y como yo
I also remember when I was seventeen years old, and how I

estuve mal antes de aprender la curandería. Vine de Lima mal. Me
was bad off before I learned curing. I came from Lima hexed. I

podría en vida, y me curó la vieja Laura. Para que la vieja,
was rotting alive, and *doña* Laura cured me. But for the old lady,

no me quedo, tomando mi cervecita.
I wouldn't be here, drinking my little beer.

El San Pedro estuvo en un vaso grandazo. ¡Todo lo amargo!
The San Pedro brew was in a huge glass. All that bitterness!

Mi mamá se asustó y mi tío Arcario también. Los
My mother was frightened, and my uncle Arcario was too. Their

ojos se lloraban. Dijeron, "¡Se muere! ¡Se muere!"
eyes were full of tears. They said, "He's dying! He's dying!"

Salió la cerveza negra. ¡Hasta la nuca! Me curó
Black beer came out—up to the nape of my neck! The old lady

la vieja, y no me cobró más que cincuenta soles. Cincuenta soles, no
cured me, and she only charged me fifty soles. Fifty soles, it's

es nada.
nothing.

Me gustaban esos trabajos, y poco a poco fuí interesándome
I liked those "works," and little by little I became interested

en la curandería. Después de que estuve con María, me invitaron a una
in curing. After I was with Maria, her relatives invited me to a

mesa. El padrino de Chochi estuvo mi maestro, pues. Mercedes
session. Chochi's godfather was my teacher then, Mercedes

Silva, un viejito con unos bigotazos. Asistí a una mesa,
Silva, a little old man with a big mustache. I helped at one

otra mesa. A mí me gustó la macana. Hizo una curación con
session after another. I liked the rattle. He did a cure with little

pomitos, pero no estaba contento con eso.
herb jars, but I wasn't content with that.

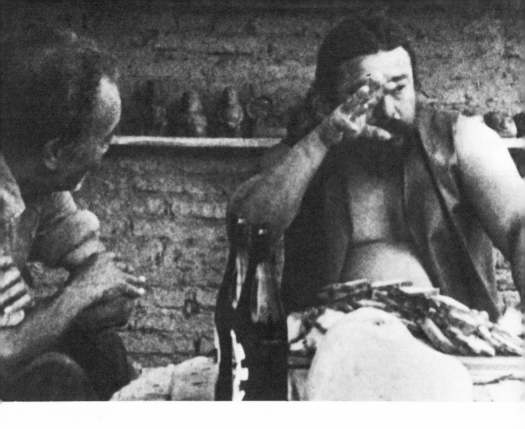

De ahí . . . me acuerdo de don Pedro Alvarez, el pintor.
From there . . . I remember *don* Pedro Alvarez, the painter. I

Conversando con él—estuvo mal un tiempo—y me dijo,
was speaking with him—he was sick for a while—and he said to

"¿Tú que conoces un poquito, que te parece si me acompáñas
me, "You who know a little, what do you think if you come with

a visitar un gran brujo, don Brigido Saavedra?" Un negro
me to visit a great sorcerer, *don* Brigido Saavedra?" A black

que parecía gorila con una caraza. Tocaba su
guy who looked like a gorilla with a huge face. He played his

guitarra y nos hizo una noche.
guitar and did a night for us.

Yo entré de alzador, cómo se llama, de rastrero. Yo
I entered as assistant, how do you say it, as "tracker." I

tomé misha por primera vez, con San Pedro. Tres dedos de
drank datura for the first time, with San Pedro. Three fingers of

misha y comencé a mirar. ¡Campeón mundial! ¡Y él con su
datura and I began to "see." A world champion! And he with his

33

guitarra . . . un tarjo de los demonios! Me gustó la cuestión, y me dijo
guitar . . . a demon's chant! I liked this business, and he told me

que si yo quería trabajar con él, parecía bien. Yo le dije,
that if I wanted to work with him, it looked good. I told him,

"Bueno, sí, le voy a contestar," pero yo no regresé, y
"Well, I'm going to let you know," but I didn't go back, and it

parece que me jodió.
looks like he hexed me.

Después, preguntaba si ya había muerto, si estaba vivo cuando
Afterwards, he asked if I had died, if I was alive when I went

regresé al sur. Entonces me llevó don Pancho Centeno. Nos invitó
back south. Then *don* Pancho Centeno guided me. He invited us

una vez, y me echaron a un hueco y comenzó él a trabajar.
one time and they threw me into a pit, and he began to work.

De repente, resultaba en el aire. Dijo, "Venga ese gordito acá,
Suddenly, I flew into the air. He said, "Bring that fat one here, I

que quiero hablar con él."
want to talk with him."

Entonces me dijo, "Tú has estado en un sitio. Se ha ido un
Then he said to me, "You have been in a place where a black

negro a tu tras con una guitarra. Es un brujo, y
guy has gone behind you with a guitar. He is a sorcerer, and he

te tiene agarrado." Por eso, me hizo una limpia, el
has you under his spell." For that, the old man did a cleansing

viejo. Me limpió y me jaló para que yo sea
for me. He cleansed me, and he pulled me to him so that I would

su rastrero de él. Por eso, yo estaba en su encanto,
be his "tracker." Because of that, I was under his enchantment,

en su cuestión
in his business.

Comencé a trabajar con Pancho Centeno. Yo salí de pescar a las ocho
I began to work for Pancho Centeno. I left fishing at eight at

de la noche; nueve y media o diez estaba yo llegando, cuando recién
night; at nine-thirty or ten I was arriving, just as he was begin-

comenzaba él a trabajar, y nunca le cobraba yo nada. Ya me iba gustando
ning to work, and I never charged him anything. I was liking it

más y más, y yo iba reuniendo mis cosas poco a poco,
more and more, and little by little I was gathering my things,

de arte en arte. Mi Cristo, primeramente. Una cruz que encontró el
artifact by artifact. My Christ, first. A cross that my grand-

padre de mi abuelo. Yo mismo he hecho mis varas. Así es como,
father's father found. I made my staffs myself. It's like begin-

cómo se llama, a comenzar estudiar. Cuando estuve ya en
ning, what shall I say, beginning to study. By the time I was in

Chan Chan, yo era maestro.
Chan Chan, I was a master.

Eso motivó una serie de progresos en mi, de leer, de
This motivated a series of developments in me to read, to

estudiar, de ir aprendiendo un poco más. Además, yo vivo acá
study, to go on learning a little more. Besides, I've lived here

veinticinco años, y por eso el mar es lo esencial. Cuando
twenty-five years, and because of this the sea is essential. When

yo trabajo, siempre espalda al mar, para que me proteja.
I work, it is always with my back to the sea, so it can protect me.

Como yo marinero, como pescador, se víncula conmigo. Yo estoy ligado
As a sailor and fisherman, it links itself with me. I am allied

a él.
with it.

Vivo así, así mi vida.
I live like this, this is my life.

EDUARDO SPEAKS OF WITCHCRAFT WITH A NEIGHBOR

THE NEIGHBOR: *¿Oye Eduardo, es cierto que las brujas vuelan?*
Hey Eduardo, is it true that witches fly?

EDUARDO: *Que las brujas vuelan, son cojudeces. Lo que vuela es el*
That witches fly, that's asinine. What flies is the

astral, el doble, el resultado de la vibración del hombre. No hay
astral body, the double, the result of the vibration of man. There

otra cosa del otro mundo. La mente es lo que hace volar.
is nothing of the other world. The mind is what makes one fly.

Eso se llama el sentido de la ubicuidad, o de la transportación
This is what's called the sense of ubiquitousness, or of transpor-

a través de la distancia, a través de la materia.
tation across distance, across matter.

Por ejemplo, yo estoy trabajando aquí en mi mesa así, pero mi mente
For example, I am working here at my *mesa*, but my mind is

está elevándose que me voy a los Estados Unidos o a Virú.
elevating itself so that I can go to the United States, or to Virú

Esa es la fuerza mental de la persona, nada más, así como
Valley. This is a person's mental force, nothing more, as well as

el elemento de la "hierba" (las pócimas que tomo) trabajando
the element of the "herb" (the potions that I drink) working

junto con ella, que le aviva "el tercer ojo," "el sexto sentido."
united with it, that activates the "third eye," the "sixth sense."

Lo que trabaja es la mente. La brujería, la hechicería, la curandería están allí.
What works is the mind. Sorcery, hexing, and curing are there.

Si no hay esto, no hay nada, pues.
Without this, there is nothing.

El brujo es un hombre sin conciencia, pero yo soy curandero,
A sorcerer is a man without conscience, but I am a healer,

no brujo. Uno cura y el otro hace daño, sin embargo, muchos
not a sorcerer. One cures and the other makes hexes, yet many

se equivocan con los términos. El daño existe porque uno es malo.
get the terms wrong. Witchcraft exists because people are bad.

Así que, si yo soy maligno digo, "Este desgraciado
Therefore, if I am malevolent and say, "That disgraceful wretch

se tiene que caer" . . . al dia próximo, porque yo he interpenetrado con
has to fall" . . . the next day, because I have penetrated his

mi fuerza mental a su psiquis, a su pensamiento, que si voltea
psyche, his thinking with my mental force, so that if he turns

acá se mata, de repente él mismo se programa
this way he kills himself, suddenly he himself programs him-

al fracaso, y tuerce acá en vez de torcer allá, y se
self into failure, and he turns here instead of there, and he is

va, se mata.
gone, he kills himself.

Uno procrea diablos cuando se comporta mal. Si usted está
One creates devils when one acts badly. If you are operating

en ese plan, cuando está jugando tejas, usted está trabajando
on this principle when you are pitching coins, you are working

con la mente a fastidiar al otro, y no lo deja
with your mind to bother your opponent and not allow him to

puntear. Eso es exactito lo que hacen la macumba en
take aim. That is exactly what's done with the *macumba* in

Brasil, lo que hacen vudú en Cuba y Haití, y aquí
Brazil, what's done with voodoo in Cuba and Haiti, and here

la brujería, la macana.
with sorcery, the rattle.

La huaca nunca va a hablar, sino cuando la mente la dé
A ruin is never going to "speak," except if one's mind gives

poder magnético, la dé fuerza. Por eso, no hay que
it magnetic power, gives it force. For this reason, we should not

confundir que el espíritu, que las sombras malas lo asustan,
confuse ourselves that the spirit, that the evil shadows, frighten

lo matan a uno. Uno se asusta; la sombra no
us, kill us. One frightens oneself; it is not the shadow that

asusta a uno.
frightens one.

EDUARDO DISCUSSES THE CURE OF LUCIANO ASMAT

Esta noche, tenemos el caso de Asmat, un muchacho que ha tenido
Tonight we have the case of Asmat, a fellow who has had

mala suerte—es decir la mala suerte nunca existe, sino que existen
bad luck—that is to say bad luck does not exist, what exists are

los factores que originan ese caso. Bueno, la limpia
the factors that originate the case. Well, the "guinea pig clean-

del cuy que le hice arrojó que era un caso de
sing" that I gave him showed he had a case of witchcraft, a

golpe de espiritismo que resulta en una serie de fracasos en
"spiritual shock" that resulted in a series of failures in his

el negocio y en el hogar. Vendió su carro y se quedó en
business and in his home. He sold his car and ended up in

la miseria, y se fué a trabajar en otro sitio con la intención
poverty, and he went to work in another place with the intention

de abandonar su familia. Más que todo, se sintió incómodo.
of abandoning his family. Most of all, he felt uncomfortable.

Tuvo la suerte de llegar por acá, y se le hizo la aplicación de la terapéutica
He was fortunate to come here, and I applied the therapy of

de la mesa. Ahora se siente tranquilo hasta cierto punto, pero en esta
the mesa. Now he feels tranquil up to a certain point, but in this

sesión se le tiene que hacer su rastreo para que así veamos como
session we have to perform a "tracking" in order to see what

nos encaminamos en el futuro, y después creo que la
path we must follow in the future, and after that I think that the

cuestión es un florecimiento para reflotarlo dentro del mar de su
matter calls for a "flowering" to float him again in the sea of his

fracaso, para que él salga adelante en toda su problemática, en su
failure, so that he can move forward on all his problems, in his

negocio y en todo lo que él ha proyectado. Un florecimiento que va
business and in all that he has projected. A flowering will have

a equivaler poner todo el pensamiento, toda la acción, para que él
the effect of focusing all his thinking, all his action, so that he

se sienta otro individuo.
feels like a new individual.

Hay tres casos de enfermedad—enfermedad natural;
There are three types of sickness—"natural" sickness;

enfermedad por brujería, por inducción mental; y un tercero
sickness from witchcraft, from mental induction; and a third

por pócima, por comida o trago—y el rastreo es nada
from potions put in food or drink—and the "tracking" is nothing

más que regresar a buscar dentro del efecto a las causas de
more than going back to look within the effects for the causes of

la enfermedad. Se hace de noche por una razón: porque el
a sickness. It is done at night for a reason: because at night the

individuo de noche, en el momento onírico, se abre el
individual, in the dream state, opens within himself the princi-

principio de transitoriedad, dejándolo receptar y
ple of "transitoriality," permitting himself to receive and

transmitir sus emociones y sus vivencias.
transmit his emotions and the experiences of his life.

¿A qué cosa miramos? La coloración del aura, que es el
What do we look at? The color of the aura, which is a reflec-

reflejo de la personalidad de la persona. Todo lo que él ha hecho
tion of the person's personality. Everything that he has done

atrás y que contribuía a enajenación, de enfermedad, de
before and which has contributed to alienation, to sickness, to

miedo, de temor, de zozobra resalta en ese momento.
fear, to apprehension, to anxiety leaps forth at that moment.

¿Por qué? Porque el San Pedro y todas las otras hierbas nos ayudan.
Why? Because the San Pedro and all the other herbs help us.

Les hacen a uno vibrar, les hacen sacar la luz. Cada persona
They make one vibrate. They make one light up. Each person

tiene una vibración especial conjuntamente con el maestro y con los
has a special vibration jointly with the master and with the

elementos que le encierra. En una sesión de curandería esta "visual"
elements that envelop him. In a curing session this "vision"

se desarrolla a través de las pócimas del San Pedro y las otras
develops by means of the potion of San Pedro and the other

hierbas.
herbs.

El cactus San Pedro juega un rol principal en estos trabajos.
The San Pedro cactus plays a principle role in this work.

En mi terapia es indispensable más que todo.
More than anything else, it is indispensable in my therapy.

Hay San Pedro de doce, de ocho, de siete, de seis, de cinco, y de
There are San Pedros of twelve, eight, seven, six, five, and of

cuatro filos. De cuatro es bien difícil a encontrar, pero aquél que encuentre
four ribs. One with four is very difficult to find, but he who finds

un San Pedro de cuatro filos, se cura todas las enfermedades y los males.
a four-ribbed San Pedro can cure all sicknesses and maladies.

El San Pedro de cuatro filos es el San Pedro místico; se usaba en
Four-ribbed San Pedro is the mystical San Pedro: it was used in

tiempos inmemoriales, y está representada en la pictografía mochica, en
time immemorial, and is depicted in Mochica pictography, in

la escultura de Chavın de Huántar, en la sierra, y aquí en la
the sculpture of Chavin de Huántar, in the Sierra, and in the

costa del norte, donde su aplicación al curanderismo es esencial
north coast region, where its application to curing is essential

hasta la actualidad.
up to the present.

En las grandes cerámicas pre-colombinas se encuentra
In the great pre-Columbian ceramics we encounter very

representaciones muy emotivas de curanderas con el San Pedro
emotional representations of female healers with the San Pedro

en la mano. El mismo chamán es importante, primordial,
in their hands. The shaman, himself, is important, primordial,

y insustituible en el campo del curanderismo. Él manipula el San
and without substitution in the field of curing. He uses the San

Pedro que toca puntos especiales de la persona, y le da
Pedro which affects special points of a person, and gives him

un "sexto sentido" de acuerdo al tópico que va a tratarse.
a "sixth sense" in accord with the topic with which he is dealing.

Tomar el San Pedro la hace resaltar a una dimensión especial.
Taking San Pedro makes him leap into a special dimension.

Eso retribuye por que los antiguos le han reflejado en sus
This explains why the ancients have reflected it in their ceram-

cerámicas y sus arquitecturas.
ics and in their architecture.

Las cerámicas son como un libro como un texto, en el cual
The ceramics are like a book, like a text, in which, through

a través de mi arte, me dió el conocimiento importante,
the medium of my art, I have been given important knowledge,

y donde yo aprendí el sinnúmero de técnicas que sean las que yo
and where I have learned the numerous techniques which I am

estoy tratando de operar. Eso me ha ayudado en gran forma para que me
now trying to apply. This has helped me a great deal so that I

conduzca a través del conocimiento de la curandería, y
can conduct myself in accord with the knowledge of curing, and

a través de mi arte; eso más que todo, me ha dado
in accord with my art; this, more than anything, has given me

el amplitud para entender la tradición de los grandes maestros.
the capacity to understand the tradition of the great masters.

Por ejemplo, eso está de acuerdo justamente con lo que significa
For example, this is precisely in accord with the meaning of

la mesa. La mesa es la parte importante de una sesión de curandería por
the *mesa*. The *mesa* is the important part of a curing session for

la sencilla razón de que es el tablero donde se computan todas las fuerzas
the simple reason that it is the panel where all the elemental

elementales. Consiste de tres campos: el Justiciero
forces are computed. It is composed of three "fields": the Field

a la derecha, el Ganadero a la izquierda, y el
of Justice to the right, the Field of Evil to the left, and the

Centro Medio. El Justiciero tiene como eje principal
Mediating Center. The Field of Justice has as its principle axis

el Cristo y todos sus santos, su séquito divino, según el
Christ and all His saints, His divine retinue according to Chris-

sincretismo religioso cristiano. El Cristo es el eje primordial que
tian religious syncretism. The Christ is the primordial axis that

mueve todo de acuerdo a mi criterio, a mi sentido,
moves everything in accord with my criteria, with my feeling,

a mi religión, más que todo a mi fé, mi pacto con Dios a
with my religion, most of all with my faith, my pact with God to

hacer el bien a la gente, y a servir a la humanidad. Yo busco siempre en el
do good to people and to serve humanity. I always look to the

Justiciero borrar todas influencias negativas.
Field of Justice to erase all negative influences.

El Ganadero es donde juegan las fuerzas elementales
The Field of Evil is where the elemental negative forces

negativas, es donde uno busca la causa de un mal. Si yo veo
hold sway, is where one looks for the cause of a problem. If I see

una enfermedad, se virtua según el síndrome dentro este
a sickness, it manifests according to its syndrome within this

campo, y cada enfermedad está "de acuerdo." Por ejemplo, si es un
field, and each sickness is in "agreement." For example, if it is a

caso de la brujería, de brebaje con hueso de muerto, entonces
case of sorcery, of a potion made of dead person's bones, then the

vibra la vara de la lechuza porque de ahí marco los cementerios, los moribundos.
owl staff vibrates, because it marks the cemeteries, the dying.

Pero si es un mal natural, hay un otro artefacto que
But if it is a natural malady, there is some other artifact that

vibra de acuerdo a lo que manda su astral. Salta cada
vibrates in accord with what the astral body mandates. Each

enfermedad, y salta a la vez el antídoto que tienes que
sickness "jumps" and at the same time the antidote you have to

utilizar. Para cada enfermedad hay una hierba fulana
use also "jumps." For each sickness there is such and such herb

que hay que darla. Para conocer eso se ha tomado el San Pedro,
that has to be given to it. To know this one has taken San Pedro,

por eso uno se ha puesto en trance y hace una introducción
for this one has put oneself in trance and made a mental and

mental y espiritual del enfermo, hacía adentro de la persona
spiritual introduction into the patient, been inside the person

para ver el mal.
to see the malady.

Todo está estabilizado por el Centro Medio que
Everything is stabilized by the Mediating Center which

computa las otras dos zonas. Es el balanceo de los otros
computes the other two zones. It is the balance of the other

campos, la estabilidad de la mesa. Como yo he dicho antes, la mesa
fields, the stability of the *mesa*. As I have said before, the *mesa*

no es más que un tablero de control para poder
is nothing more than a control panel by which one is able to

calibrar la infinidad de asequibles de cada persona. Las varas son
calibrate the infinity of accesses into each person. The staffs are

artefactos, herramientas que la dan a uno fuerza. Esa fuerza las da
artifacts, tools that give one force. This force is given to them by

el maestro, el operador, mediante su poder bioelectromagnético.
the master, the operator, by means of his bioelectromagnetic

El le da potencialidad a la vara, entonces vibra justamente
power. He gives potentiality to the staff, then it vibrates pre-

porque el paciente tiene un mal. La vara está ajustada
cisely because the patient has a malady. The staff is adjusted

según la cuenta, a la razón de la enfermedad. Es una
according to the "account," the reason for the sickness. It is a

herramienta, nada más.
tool, nothing more.

Los dos alzadores, los rastreadores, han sido la conexión
The two assistants, the "trackers," make the connection

entre el paciente y el maestro, el dínamo de acción.
between the patient and the master, the generator of action.

Ellos son cordónes umbilicales para el factor energético que soy como
They are umbilical cords for the energy factor that I am as

el dínamo. Captamos, nosotros tres, cual es la razón de esta enfermedad. El
generator. We three capture the reason for the sickness. The

milagro está acá: el poder de la mente involucrando la fuerza
miracle is here: the power of the mind introducing the bioelec-

bioelectromagnético del hombre como operador dentro del campo de la curación.
tromagnetic force of man as operator into the field of curing.

No crea que solamente sentándose el curandero, cantando,
One should not think that only by sitting singing, occasion-

emitiendo un tarjo, se logre hacer una curación. Siempre a la
ally emitting a chant, that the curer effects a cure. Always at the

apertura de una sesión yo tengo que meditarlo mucho, hilando
beginning of a session I have to meditate a great deal, spinning

una serie de problemas actuales relacionados a quien voy a curar.
a series of actual problems related to whom I am going to cure.

Jamás hacer una curación como, "Ya te voy a curar
One must never perform a cure like, "I am going to cure you

y punto," al paso. No, tiene que programarlo: primeramente,
now, period," on the run. No, it has to be programmed: first of

por el diagnóstico, mediante la limpia del cuy. Después,
all, by the diagnosis, through the guinea pig cleansing. After

uno escoje el día que va uno a operar de
that, one chooses the day on which one is going to operate in

acuerdo a la secuencia astral, de la luna más que todo. Con
accord with the astral sequence, of the moon most of all. With

eso, se comienza de acuerdo a las enseñanzas, el criterio
this, one begins in accord with the teachings, the numerological

numerológico. Por esa razón se canta desde las diez hasta las doce de la noche.
criterion. For this reason one sings from ten until midnight.

La curación es a la una, el principio, la
The cure is from one in the morning, the beginning, the

génesis del día, hasta las tres o las cuatro de la mañana. A las seis
genesis of the day, until three or four in the morning. At six in

se termina todo. Las seis es la apertura del
the morning everything terminates. Six is the opening of the

nuevo día. A este momento se cierre el tercer ojo porque ahora
new day. At this moment the "third eye" closes because it is now

la fuerza del sol da su florecimiento, en el mismo sentido que hizo el San
that the force of the sun flowers, in the same sense as did the San

Pedro, que floreció en la noche, dando su propia luz, su energía
Pedro, which bloomed in the night, giving its own light, its own

vital. Todo esto entonces es justamente lo que a mi me llama a pensar, a
vital energy. All this then is precisely what calls me to think, to

prepararme para que yo llegue a un fin feliz en cada obra.
prepare myself so that I will arrive at a happy end in each work.

Porque no es cuestión de hacer nada más cosas para
Because it is not just a matter of doing things just for the sake of

hacer. ¡Siempre preparando!
doing them. One is always preparing!

47

Lo que hacemos los curanderos actualmente estamos dando
Actually, what we *curanderos* are doing is giving guide-

pautas al paciente sobre sus problemas. Siempre de acuerdo
lines to the patient in regard to his problems. Always in accord

a sus creencias, su religión particularmente, sea cual fuere, porque
with his beliefs, particularly his religion, whatever it may be,

todas la religiones se encaminan hacia un punto que es Dios. Muchos lo
because all religions lead to a point which is God. Many think of

llaman a Dios como pintan los cristianos: un señor barbudo con
God the way the Christians depict him: as a bearded man with

un mundo en la mano. A otros en otra forma. Pero Dios es la
the world in his hand. Others in other forms. But God is the

energía cósmica imbuida en uno mismo. Sí, somos parte de Dios,
cosmic energy within ourselves. Yes, we are part of God

porque tenemos esa energía, y esta energía es una fuerza
because we have that energy, and this energy is an elemental

elemental para que así nosotros podemos convergir a un punto importante, que
force that allows us to converge at an important point, which

es la curación.
is curing.

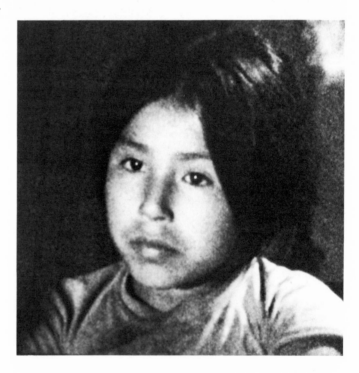

THE CURING SESSION FOR LUCIANO ASMAT

Raising the Mesa in General
With the Seven Thousand Accounts

En las siete mil cuentas,
With the seven thousand accounts,

Poderosas, curanderas, justicieras:
Powerful, curing, justifying:

Señor mio Santísimo, en tu Santo Nombre,
My Lord, Most Holy, in Your Sainted Name,

Con tu santísima luz y poder,
With Your Holy light and power,

Sigo levantando, pagando, floreciendo, justificando,
I continue raising, paying, flowering, justifying,

Todos sus encantos y sus poderes,
All Your enchantments and Your powers.

Y a los presentes en todas las acciones,
And for those present in all their activities,

Sigo levantando,
I continue raising,

Parando toda su cuenta.
Bringing up all of your account.

Así voy contando,
In this way, I go accounting,

Las siete justicias de mi Señor,
The Seven Miracles of my Lord,

Los siete Angeles, los siete Espíritus,
The seven Angels, the seven Spirits,

Las siete Iglesias del Mundo,
The seven Churches of the World,

Los tres clavos y los cuatro Evangelistas,
The three nails and the four Evangelists.

Bien contado, para glorificarte,
Well accounted, in order to glorify,

En todo su encanto y poder.
You in all Your enchantment and power.

En todo el arte de la cuenta,
With all the art of the account,

En todas sus hierberias y poderes,
With all Your herbs and powers,

En su gloria,
With Your glory,

Así voy levantando.
Thus I go raising.

Cristo, Señor Santísimo, Divino Maestro,
Christ, Holy Lord, Divine Master,

Ilumina con tu luz y tu poder nuestras mentes,
Illuminate our minds with Your light and power,

Toda su bondad infinita,
All Your Infinite Goodness,

En nuestras artes y curaciones.
In our arts and cures.

50

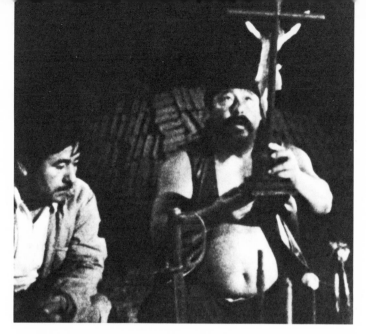

Bendice a todos los presentes y ausentes.
Bless all those present and absent.

Amén.
Amen.

Raising the Field of Good With the Twelve Thousand Accounts and the Chant of Jesus

En mi ciento con las doce mil cuentas,
In my game with the twelve thousand accounts,

Voy levantando:
I go raising:

En un pesebre bendito,
In a blessed stable,

Y entre la mula y el buey,
And between the mule and the ox,

Y en la estrella luminosa,
And with the luminous star,

Vienen contando.
They come accounting.

Los tres Reyes Magos,
The Three Wise Men,

Adorando con su canto,
Worshipping with their song.

Melchor, Gaspar, y Baltazár,
Melchior, Gaspar, and Balthazar,

Vienen con oro, incienso, y mirra,
Come with gold, frankincense, and myrrh.

Divino Jesús, redentor del mundo entero,
Divine Jesus, Redeemer of the entire world,

A los doce años ya entre los doctores de la ley,
At twelve years of age among the doctors of the law,

Discutiendo grandes obras y contando,
Discussing great works and accounting,

Y en los encantos viene jugando.
And with the enchantments He comes playing.

A los treinta años en su gran canto,
At thirty years of age with His great song,

Viene ya con sus potentos,
He comes with His great potency,

En sus milagros en el Monte de las Bienaventuranzas,
With His miracles on the Mount of the Beatitudes.

Y en el lavatorio de manos de Pilatos,
And with the washing of the hands of Pilate,

Con su cruz a cuestas,
With His cross on His shoulders,

Viene ya.
He comes now,

Y en la calle,
And in the street,

Los dolores por la Virgen, Madre Santa,
The pains of the Virgin, Holy Mother,

Y los doce.
And the twelve.

Con sus siete caídas,
With His seven falls,

Con su corazón doliente.
With His suffering heart of pain.

Y en el Monte Calvario, su carne hiriente,
And on Mount Calvary, His wounded flesh,

Y entre el buen ladrón, San Dimas,
And between the good thief, Saint Dimas,

Y entre el mal ladrón,
And between the bad thief,

Vienen crucificando al Señor Cristo,
They come crucifying Christ the Lord,

Redentor del mundo entero,
Redeemer of the entire world.

Y a la hora,
And at the hour,

Y entre truenos y relámpagos, temblores,
And between thunder and lightning, earthquakes

Se raja el manto del Cielo.
The veil of Heaven is torn,

Y entregando el alma al Padre,
And delivering His Soul to the Father,

Ya viene entregando,
He comes delivering,

Ya viene contando,
He comes accounting,

En su caridad y su bondad y su perdón,
With His charity and His kindness and His forgiveness.

Resuscita al tercer día dentro de los muertos.
Resurrected on the third day from among the dead,

Y triunfante de su ciento.
And triumphant in His game,

Jesús viene resucitando en su encanto.
Jesus comes resurrected with His enchantment,

Y va jugando y pagando y levantando.
And goes playing, and paying, and raising.

Y así viene Jesús lindo,
And thus beautiful Jesus,

Viene, triunfante reinando.
Comes reigning triumphant.

Y subiendo en su nube blanca,
And ascending on His white cloud,

Viene, poderoso y triunfante,
He comes, powerful and triumphant,

En su gloria.
In His glory,

Y en su hermosa venia,
And with His beautiful forgiveness,

Y a la derecha del Señor Padre Poderoso Eterno,
And to the right of the powerful Eternal Father,

Viene contando.
He comes accounting.

Gloria al Señor, gloria.
Glory to the Lord. Glory.

Amén.
Amen.

Raising the Mediating Center and the Field of Evil With the Twenty-five Thousand Accounts and the Chant of the Ancients

Con Cipriano poderoso,
With powerful Saint Cyprian,

Cabalista y cirujano, viejo caminante
Cabbalist and surgeon, old traveler,

Y en los cuatro vientos y los cuatro caminos,
And with the four winds and the four roads,

Y en las veinticinco mil cuentas,
And with the twenty-five thousand accounts,

Justicieras, curanderas, y ganaderas,
Good, curing, and evil,

Ajustando con mis buenos rambeadores, mis sorbedores.
Adjusting with my good assistants, my absorbers.

Con buenas cuentas.
With good accounts,

Así vengo parando,
Thus I come raising,

En todo su encanto y su poder:
With all his enchantment and his power:

Cerro Blanco, Cerro Colorado,
White Mountain, Red Mountain,

Cerro Chaparri, Cerro Yanahuanga,
Mount Chaparri, Mount Yanahuanga,

Cerro Chalpón, poderoso y bendito,
Mount Chalpón, powerful and blessed,

Con tu volcanazo de fuego ardiendo,
With your great volcano of burning fire,

Donde cuenta el encanto del Padre Guatemala.
Where the enchantment of Father Guatemala is accounted,

Y en sus grandes poderes,
And with your great powers,

Todos sus encantos voy llamando,
All his enchantments I go calling,

Voy contando.
I go accounting.

Cerro Pelagato, Cerro Huascarán,
Pelagato Mountain, Mount Huascarán,

Cerro del Ahorcado, Cerro Campanario,
Hanged Man's Mountain, Belfry Mountain,

Cerro Cuculicote y su gran poder,
Cuculicote Mountain and its great power,

Donde vengo ajustando,
Where I come adjusting,

Y a mi banco,
And at my bench,

En todos sus encantos y poderes,
With all its enchantments and powers,

Voy contando.
I go accounting.

Y en mi buena laguna encantada,
And with my good enchanted lagoon,

Mi Huaringana,
My Huaringana,

Donde voy llamando.
Where I go calling,

Mi buena Laguna Shimbe,
My good Shimbe Lagoon,

Siempre linda y poderosa,
Always beautiful and powerful,

Donde juega mi maestro Florentino García,
Where my master Florentino Garcia plays,

En su gran poder del chamán,
With his great power as a shaman.

Y así vengo contando,
And thus I come accounting,

Con todos mis encantos,
With all my enchantments.

Vara por vara,
Staff by staff,

Cerro por cerro,
Mountain by mountain,

Laguna por laguna,
Lagoon by lagoon,

Y en el chorro de Santo Crisanto,
And in the Stream of Santo Crisanto,

Voy llamando.
I go calling.

En mis hermosos jardines bien floridos,
With my beautiful flowery gardens,

Con todas sus hierbas y sus encantos,
With all their herbs and their enchantments,

Voy llamando.
I go calling.

Cuenta por cuenta, voy jugando,
Account by account, I go playing,

Y en mi Huaca poderosa de los Gentiles,
And with my powerful Temple of the Ancients.

Donde voy contando, jugando, floreciendo.
Where I go accounting, playing, flowering.

Huaca Prieta, Huaca del Sol, y Huaca de la Luna,
Huaca Prieta, Temple of the Sun, and Temple of the Moon,

Juega a mi ciento.
Play at my game.

Con la hierba del hombre,
With the herb of man,

Con la hierba del león,
With the herb of the lion,

Con la hierba de la coqueta,
With the herb of the coquette,

Voy cantando.
I go singing.

Con mis buenos hierbateros voy llamando,
With my good herbalists I go calling,

Todos los poderes y los encantos,
All the powers and the enchantments,

Que mi buen remedio viene ya,
So that my good remedy comes now,

Buscando, justificando, levantando, parando,
Looking, justifying, raising, standing up.

Con sus buenos encantos.
With their good enchantments,

Todos los grandes maestros,
All the great masters,

Van contando donde cuento.
Go accounting where I account.

A las doce de la noche entera,
At twelve midnight,

Y a la madrugada,
And at dawn,

Seis de la mañana al ojo del sol,
Six in the morning under the eye of the sun,

Voy llamando,
I go calling,

Estoy contando y refrescando,
I am accounting and refreshing.

Buena hora, buenos vientos,
Good time, good winds,

Voy llamando y contando,
I go calling and accounting,

De mis buenas maravillas,
With my good marvels,

Vengo levantando todo mi banco.
I come raising all of my bench,

Donde cuentan todos los grandes poderosos.
Where all the great powers are accounted,

Voy dominando todo golpe,
I go dominating all spiritual shocks,

Floreciendo en buena hora.
Flowering in good time.

Call to the Staffs

Junto a mis varas y mi cuenta,
Together with my staffs and my account,

Y en mi banco gloria,
And at my heavenly bench,

Señor Hombre Cristo Santo,
Lord Holy Christ,

Voy contando mis varas y en mi paseo.
I go accounting my staffs and on my walk.

Cuentan mis prendas,
Account my tokens,

Cuentan mis acerros,
Account my steels,

Cuentan mis varas y todo mi ciento:
Account my staffs and my whole game:

Juega mi espada San Miguel Arcángel,
Play my Sword of Saint Michael the Archangel,

¡Cuenta y bendice!
Account and bless!

Con su fé,
With his faith,

El fuego ardiente,
The burning fire,

Viene chicoteando adentro los cuatro vientos,
He comes lashing in the four winds,

¡Juega!
Play!

Todos los demonios y todos los diablos,
I go overturning,

Los vengo volteando.
All the demons and all the devils,

Con mi buena espada.
With my good sword,

Ahora viene.
That comes now,

Contando y justificando.
Accounting and justifying.

¡Juega mi espada hermosa de mi buen San Pablo!
Play my beautiful Sword of good Saint Paul!

En las tribunas va cobrando,
In the tribunals he goes collecting,

Y en su buen encanto como justiciero,
And with his good enchantment as a righteous man,

Como curandero cuenta,
As a healer he accounts.

Y buen soldado,
And good soldier,

Vengo con él jugando y justificando,
I come with him, playing and justifying,

Parando en este mi banco.
Raising at this my bench,

¡Juega mis poderes!
Play my powers!

¡*Juega ya mi vara Virgen de las Mercedes!*
Play now my Staff Virgin of Mercy!

Y en sus grandes armerías,
And with her great armories,

La vengo jugando,
I come playing it.

Vengo pues llamando.
I come now calling,

Todos los soldados y todos sus encantos,
All the soldiers and all their enchantments,

¡*Juegan en su ciento!*
Play at her game!

Pura y santa con sus buenos venablos,
Pure and holy with her great darts,

Buenas lanzas al diestre,
Good lances on her right hand,

Viene ahora jugando,
She comes now playing,

Y en mi ciento voy contando.
And in my game I go accounting.

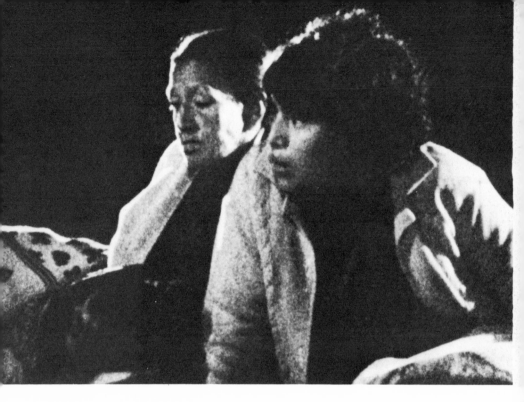

¡Cuenta mi vara chupaflores!
Account my Hummingbird Staff!

Jugando en sus grandes hierberías,
Playing in their great herb gardens,

Los chupaflores juntan,
The hummingbirds gather,

Todos los dolores malos y enfermedades,
All the bad pains and sicknesses,

Juegan con sus encantos.
They play with their enchantments.

El pajarillo pinto.
The speckled bird,

Trabajando desde el Paraguay a la Guatemala,
Working from Paraguay to Guatemala,

Y en su canto en su tiempo,
And with its song in its time,

Florido mi encanto.
Flowering my enchantment,

Juega mi cuenta.
It plays with my account.

61

¡Juega mi vara galgo sanguino!
Play my sanguine Greyhound Staff!

Viene pues el alcosunco,
Now comes the spotted dog,

Y en los grandes pedregales,
And in great rocky places,

Y entre los agileñas espinales,
And between the keen spines,

En arenales vecinales,
In nearby sandy places,

Y entre los juncos y laderas,
And between the reeds and slopes,

Viene pues ahora rasgando,
He comes now tearing,

De todos los males del cuerpo,
All the maladies of the body,

Que se llena el alma entero.
That fill the entire soul.

Juega mi gran perdiguero,
Play my great pointer,

Y bebiendo en su hermoso chorro el Sapamé,
And drinking in its beautiful steam, the Sapamé,

En la Huaringa, te encuentro.
In the Huaringa I find you.

¡Juega mi vara águila!
Play my Eagle Staff!

Chillada la cuenta poderosa del Everest,
Screech the powerful account of Everest,

En los Andes vienen Huascarán, Huandóy,
In the Andes come Huascarán, Huandóy,

Chimborazo,
Chimborazo,

Pelagato, y Misti,
Pelagato, and Misti,

Con sus grandes cuentas.
With their great accounts.

Cuenta mi águila real en su bravura,
Account my royal eagle with its bravery,

Y con los lábaros romanos juega.
And with Roman pennants it plays.

¡Juega mi águila real!
Play my royal eagle!

En su poder y su gloria,
With its power and its glory,

De sus triunfos,
With its triumphs,

Voy llamando.
I go calling.

¡Juega pues mi vara hermosa pico de pez espada!
Play now my beautiful Swordfish Beak Staff!

Cuenta la ballena, el tiburón, y el delfín,
Account the whale, the shark, and the dolphin,

Jugando en las bahías y puertos,
Playing in the bays and ports,

En los mares, arrecifes, buenos golfos,
In the seas, reefs, good gulfs,

Y entre los grandes barcos.
And among the great ships.

Cuentan trombas marinas y tempestades,
Account marine waterspouts and tempests,

Juegan granizales, ventarrones, y neblinas.
Play hailstorms, great winds, and fogs.

Gente que juegan en los mares,
People who play on the seas,

Ahora sus almas perdidos se van encontrados.
Now their lost souls are being found.

¡Juega mi vara serpiente!
Play my Serpent Staff!

Cuenta con San Cipriano,
Account with Saint Cyprian,

Quien desde los primeros años,
Who from the first years,

Ya jugaba con los Reyes Magos,
Played with the Three Wise Men,

Y con Moisés y Solomón.
And with Moses and Solomon.

Cabalista, cirujano, viejo caminante,
Cabbalist, surgeon, old traveler,

¡En su encanto, bien parada!
With his enchantment, well raised!

Mi culebra de bronce,
My bronze snake,

En grandes poderes jugando entre viborones.
With great powers playing among vipers.

La shushupe, silbacocha, la mococha,
The bushmaster, silbacocha, the mococha,

Con ojillos grandes vienan parando.
With big eyes they come raising,

Y en sus lenguas van contando,
And with their tongues they go accounting,

Jugando y reptando.
Playing and crawling,

Floreciendo los poderes.
Flowering the powers.

Juega mi vara señorita,
Play my Señorita Staff,

Hermosa hierbatera y poderosa,
Beautiful herbalist and powerful,

Serrana de la Huaringana.
Highlander from the Huaringana.

Entra mi hija,
Enter my daughter,

Con tu buen encanto,
With your good enchantment,

Y tu hornamo-lirio lindo,
And your beautiful lily-herb,

Y enamorada, con tu rosa roja al pecho,
And in love, with your red rose on your breast,

Tu rueca de hilo y tu ganadito,
Your spindle of thread and your little flocks,

Vienes ya contando,
You come now accounting,

Y enredando los amores.
And entangling love affairs.

En tu encanto hierbatero y tu tamborcita,
With your herbal enchantment and your little drum,

Serrana linda en tu cerro encantado,
Pretty highlander with your enchanted mountain,

64

Resguardando las lagunas con la Shimbe reinando,
Guarding the lagoons with Shimbe reigning,

¡Juega pues, en buena hora!
Play now, in good time!

Y ahora cuenta mi vara lechuzón,
And now account my Owl Staff,

¡Los siete mil cementerios,
The seven thousand cemeteries,

Los mortuorios, los moribundos, y gentiles!
The funerals, the dying, and the ancients!

En las casas y los castillos abandonados.
In the abandoned houses and castles,

Donde voy jugando,
Where I go playing,

Con los shusheques y las paupacas,
With the buzzards and the owls.

En las iglesias derribadas y huacas,
In demolished churches and temple ruins,

Todas los almas, encontrados y enredados,
All the souls, found and entangled,

Ya los vengo yo llamando,
Now I come calling them,

Desligando, desenredando.
Unbinding, untangling.

En los encantos de hipnotismo y sugestión,
In the enchantments of hypnotism and suggestion,

Voy contando,
I go accounting,

¡En buena hora y en mi banco!
In good time and at my bench!

¡Juega mi vara de Satanás!
Play my Staff of Satan!

Voy parando los santos negros,
I go raising the black saints,

Los demonios, malas sombras, malos vientos,
The demons, bad shadows, bad winds,

Los duendes y las fantasmas, espíritus malignos,
The goblins and ghosts, malignant spirits,

Donde juegan y en sus cientos,
Where they play and in their games,

En el Cerro Guañape y el Bolsillo del Diablo,
In Cerro Guañape and Devil's Pocket Mountain.

Todos sus encantos cuentan con Lucifer,
All their enchantments account with Lucifer,

Pero ya los vengo dominando,
But I come now dominating them,

Con la vara de San Miguel Arcángel,
With the staff of Saint Michael the Archangel,

Y así va jugando Cristo,
And thus Christ goes playing,

Justificando y abriendo el sendero,
Justifying and opening the path,

¡En buena hora!
In good time!

Purifying the Curandero
With the Chant of Eduardo

Voy dando un buen encanto,
I go along giving a good enchantment,

Un buen remedio de mi banco:
A good remedy from my bench:

San Cipriano,
Saint Cyprian,

Quien desde los primeros años,
Who from the first years,

Ya jugaba dentro del encanto,
Already played within the enchantment,

Con los Reyes Magos,
With the Three Wise Men.

Cabalista y cirujano,
Cabbalist and surgeon,

Con mi buen San Pedro,
With my good San Pedro,

Todos los brebajes,
All the potions,

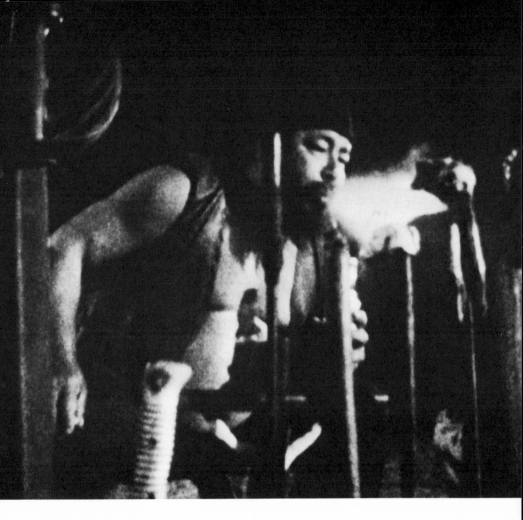

De hueso de muerto, gentiles,
Of dead man's bones, ancients,

Polvo de culebra, antimonio, y minerales,
Snake powder, antimony, and minerals,

Todos se cuentan.
All are accounted.

Todos los dolores del cuerpo entero,
All the ailments of the entire body,

Todos los golpes de espiritismo, hipnotismo, sugestión,
All spiritual shocks, hypnotism, suggestion,

Todos se cuentan.
All are accounted.

67

San Cipriano con chungana en mano,
Saint Cyprian with rattle in hand,

Y su vaso con el remedio,
And his glass with the remedy,

Bien purificado,
Well purified,

El contaba en sus grandes tiempos,
He accounted in his great times,

Desde la Huaringana voy jugando,
From the Huaringana I go playing,

Curandero, justiciero,
Curer, justifier,

Y en mi ciento,
And at my game,

Donde se cuenta la Shimbe hermosa,
Where beautiful Shimbe is accounted,

¡Juega!
Play!

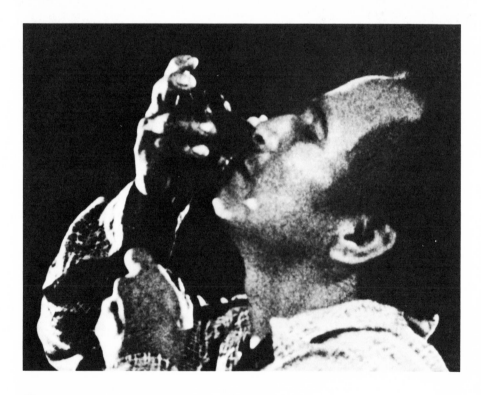

The Tracking of Luciano Asmat

Luciano Asmat,
Luciano Asmat,

Tu nombre y tu apellido,
Your name and your surname,

Por tu rastro y por tu sombra,
For your track and for your shadow,

En mi banco gloria grande,
At my great heavenly bench,

Luciano Asmat vente,
Luciano Asmat come,

Vamos a ver que vara . . .
Let us see which staff . . .

Ya entrada. Cuenta ya mi vara de la Virgen de las Mercedes. Sus
Now it has entered. My Virgin of Mercy Staff accounts. Its

encantos cuentan con todos sus bienes. Juega, la Virgen de
enchantments account with all their goodness. Play, Virgin of

las Mercedes con todos sus armerías, sus gentes, y sus oraciones; con
Mercy with all her armories, her people, and her prayers; with

todos sus triunfos. Con mi vara de la Virgen de las Mercedes, voy
all her triumphs, With my Staff of the Virgin of Mercy, I go

contando.
accounting.

Yo vengo parando, levantando, justificando con su buen
I come standing, raising, justifying with your good enchant-

encanto. Cuenta y descuenta y desmarca trancas y volteadas,
ment. Account and discount and undo barriers and bad turns,

y malas sombras, y inconvenientes, y mala suerte, y todos los
and evil shadows, and inconveniences, and bad luck, and all

fracasos. Luz, llamando por la Virgen poderosa de las Mercedes:
failures. Light, I come calling for the powerful Virgin of Mercy:

Luciano Asmat,
Luciano Asmat,

Curandero justiciero,
Curandero of Justice,

Voy levantando tu nombre y tu apellido,
I come raising your name, your surname,

En mi vara poderosa,
With my powerful staff,

Y en las grandes armerías
And with the great armories,

Y en los siete poderes,
And with the seven powers,

Voy contando y parando,
I go accounting and standing,

Floreciendo.
Flowering.

En la Laguna Shimbe hermosa poderosa,
With the beautiful and powerful Shimbe Lagoon,

Donde cuenta Florentino García,
Where Florentino Garcia accounts,

Mi maestro.
My master,

Y en su nombre y en su encanto,
And with his name and with his enchantment,

Y en sus hierbas encantadoras,
And with his enchanted herbs,

Voy jugando.
I go playing,

Floreciendo y endulzando tu camino.
Flowering and sweetening your path.

Voy desmarcando y cruzando,
I go undoing and crossing,

Todo encono, todo collo, toda tranca,
All rancor, all cowardice, all barriers,

Inconvenientes en tu vida,
Inconveniences in your life,

Y en tu camino,
And in your path,

En el hogar y en el trabajo,
In the home and at work.

Te vengo contando, pagando, y marcando,
I come accounting, paying, and marking you,

Justificando en buena hora,
Justifying in good time,

Tus acciones y tus proyecciones.
Your actions and your projections.

Voy llamando la Fuente de San Cipriano,
I go calling the Fountain of Saint Cyprian,

Poderoso y ayudando,
Powerful and helping,

Y con la cuenta de la Virgen de las Mercedes,
And with the account of the Virgin of Mercy,

Voy jugando y trabajando.
I go playing and working.

The Account of Luciano Asmat

Hierba, entra a mi cuenta, voy llamando:
Herb, enter into my account, I go calling:

Veo todavia un carro que se hunde en una huaca. Se va de frente
I still see a car that is sinking into a ruin. It goes straight in

como si lo comiera ya. Pero esas cosas que te sentiste, los ruidos
as if it were being eaten. But those things that you felt, the ugly

feos, los olores feos en la casa, los malos sueños de tu
noises, the ugly odors in the house, the bad dreams of your

hija, todos van a pasar. Tú vas a reaccionar, vas a
daughter, everything will pass. You are going to react, you are

salir a flote de las cosas, en buena forma, contento
going to come out afloat, on top of things, in great form, content

y tranquilo; más ligero, con más ánimo en tu trabajo.
and tranquil; lighter, with more zest for your work.

The Flowering of Luciano Asmat

Ahora viene el florecimiento.
Now comes the flowering!

Te vamos a dar energía a parar.
We are going to give you energy to stand up,

A reforzarte:
To reinforce you:

Luciano Asmat,
Luciano Asmat,

Tu nombre protegido,
Your protected name,

Vengo contra remalazo,
I come against all evil,

Vengo jugando en dulzura,
I come playing with sweetness,

Por tu rastro, por tu sombra,
For your track, for your shadow.

Mano por mano,
Hand by hand,

Pierna por pierna,
Leg by leg,

Coyuntura por coyuntura,
Joint by joint,

Sentido por sentido,
Sense by sense,

En buena hora,
In good time,

¡Te vengo levantando!
I come raising you!

Bien florido en Shimbe,
Well flowered in Shimbe,

Dominando todos los encantos y los males,
Dominating all enchantments and evils,

Bien levantado en tu vida,
Well raised in your life,

En tu empresa, en tu trabajo, en tu hogar,
In your enterprise, in your work, in your home,

En todas tus acciones y proyecciones,
In all your actions and projections,

¡Y en tu camino!
And on your path!

Así yo vengo refrescando mi banco,
Thus I come refreshing my bench,

En gloria y poder,
In glory and power,

¡Florida!
Flowered!

Cinco días tienes que permanecer en una dieta especial para que
For five days you need to stay on a special diet so that you

puedes levantarte. Cinco días de dieta, sin papar, porque
can raise yourself. Five days of diet without snacking, because

la hierba que te voy a dar es muy fuerte. No comes carne de chancho,
the herb I am going to give you is very strong. Do not eat pork,

ni frito de carne, y nada de condimentos, té o café. Nada de
nor fried meat, and no condiments, tea, or coffee. Nothing of

esas cosas, y bañarte a las seis todos los días,
these things, and you must bathe at six in the morning every

no tener cólera, no fumar, y no te vayas a la candela
day, not get angry, not smoke, and do not go near an open fire

tampoco, quédate lejos.
either, stay far away.

Pero ahora tú estás mejor. Tú ya te sientes más distinto, otro
But you are better now. You now feel different, your face has

color de cara. Antes estabas todo amarillo, estabas fregado. Tú has
color. Earlier you were all yellow, all washed out. You have

superado mucho y tienes más fuerza; hecho lo que se
overcome much and are much stronger; all that one could do

ha podido. Quizás otra oportunidad, nos agarramos
has been done. Perhaps on another occasion, we can pull it

nuevamente, pero hay que tener un poco de cuidado,
together again, but in the meantime you should just be a little

nada más. Es una cuestión de uno mismo, pero por lo menos
careful, nothing more. That is a matter for yourself, but for now

se ha hecho algo. Qué te vaya bien.
something has been done. May all go well with you.

Closing of the Account

Vengo cerrando la cuenta,
I come closing the account,

Entra mi encanto:
Enter my enchantment:

Así vengo parando en toda mi realidad,
Thus I come raising in all my reality,

Y en mi jardín,
And in my herb garden,

¡Floreciendo mi ciento!
Flowering my game!

En buena hora,
In good time,

Y a los cuatro vientos,
And to the four winds,

Vengo volteando mi cuenta,
I come turning over my account,

Chicoteando como buen guardián,
Lashing like a good guardian,

Alrededor de mi laguna,
Around my lagoon,

La Shimbe, hermosa y poderosa,
The beautiful and powerful Shimbe,

Contra toda golpeada, contrariada,
Against all shocks and contrarieties,

Y justificando.
And justifying.

Cristo purísimo,
Purest Christ,

Santo Señor, todopoderoso,
Holy Lord, All Powerful,

Gracias por haberme traído con buenas formas,
Thank you for having brought me safely,

Hasta este momento,
To this moment,

Con toda la potencia, protección, y amparo,
With all the potency, protection, and support,

De los presentes y de los ausentes.
Of those present and of those absent.

Te ruego Señor,
I beseech you Lord,

Que perdones mis pecados,
To forgive my sins,

Levanta a los caídos, a los afligidos,
Raise the fallen, the afflicted,

Y ensalza a los justos,
And exalt the just.

Señor, gracias os doy,
Lord, I give Thee thanks,

Por sanctificar mi ciento,
For sanctifying my game.

Paz a todos los hombres en este mundo,
Peace to all men in this world,

Por el poderoso Jesús Santísimo,
By the powerful Holy Jesus,

El Maestro Divino.
The Divine Master.

Así voy de su ciento,
Thus I go from His game,

Señor mio Santísimo y todos los santos,
My Holy Lord and all the saints,

Amén.
Amen.

THE CEREMONY OF HEALING

This outline of Eduardo's curing ceremony is based upon explanations he gave Douglas Sharon of sessions which were conducted and tape recorded in the summer of 1970. These explanations were augmented by other sessions and explanations taped in the fall of 1971, the winter of 1974, and the winter of 1978. From comparisons of Eduardo's activities with the rituals of other *curanderos,* we know that songs and whistling accompanied by a rattle, "raising" the *San Pedro* brew and other substances including *tabaco* (see *The Mesa Artifacts*), orally spraying perfumes, and reciting Catholic prayers in conjunction with traditional chants are all typical features of northern Peruvian *curanderismo.*

Charging the Mesa

1. *Apertura de la cuenta* (opening of the account): Eduardo sets up the *mesa* in a special order: first, the *Campo Justiciero* artifacts; second, the *Centro Medio* artifacts; third, the *Campo Ganadero* artifacts; and last, the staffs from right to left. Then, while invoking the forces of nature along with the four winds and four roads, he fills his mouth with sugar and Tabu, and he sprays the mixture three times over the *mesa* to purify it. After a second invocation, this same operation is repeated three times with sugar and *agua florida.* This is followed by another invocation and three more blasts of spray composed of sugar and *agua cananga.* Finally, sugar and sweet-lime juice are sprayed three times over the *mesa.* (Usually the total number of blasts is twelve).

2. *Oraciones* (prayers) to the *Campo Justiciero* addressing God, the Virgin Mary, and the saints of the Roman Catholic faith. These prayers, mostly in Spanish with a little Latin and some Quechua, include the Hail Mary and the Our Father.

3. *Llamada* (call) to the sacred mountains and lagoons, the ancient shrines, and to *curanderos,* alive and dead, so that they will attend the session in spirit. This call is made by a *tarjo,* or chant, which starts with Eduardo rhythmically shaking the *chungana,* or rattle. After a rhythm is established, he then whistles in time to the beat, and then he chants or breaks into a song, still shaking the *chungana.* Toward the end of the *tarjo,* he resumes whistling, ending by once again shaking the *chungana* by itself.

4. The raising *(levantada)* of the *mesa* in general *con las siete mil cuentas* (with the seven thousand accounts). After another series of prayers, mainly from within the realm of Roman Catholicism,

Eduardo "raises" the *mesa* with *tabaco* (imbibes *tabaco* through his nostrils). This is done seven times (for the seven "justices" of Christ—seven important events in the life of Christ); each time a whole shell is emptied and a short invocation is given. During this raising, Eduardo holds the Dagger of Saint Michael, the crucifix, and the rattle above his head. When he is finished, each assistant also imbibes one shellful of the same liquid. Not one drop of *tabaco* must be spilled, for if it is, the person doing the raising must start over again. This operation activates the crucifix, the axis of the *mesa*.

5. Call to all the *encantos justicieros* (good charms). Eduardo sings a *tarjo* addressed to personages of the Christian tradition—Jesus, the Virgin Mary, the apostles, saints, and angels—and to the miraculous events in their lives.

6. Raising *con las doce mil cuentas* (with the twelve thousand accounts). Eduardo invokes the twelve thousand accounts while either abstaining from or raising *tabaco*. He then pours one shell of *tabaco* for each assistant to raise. This operation activates the forces of good within the *Campo Justiciero*.

7. *Tarjo* relating the birth, life, death, and resurrection of Jesus, and the beginnings of the early Church. It is intended to invoke His presence in spirit.

8. Call and petition to God. Eduardo imitates the consecration of the mass by raising a mixture of Holy Water and Tabu above his head and then drinking it. This act is followed by his putting Tabu in his mouth, and then spraying the crucifix three times. This ends the liturgical acts between the *curandero* and God.

9. Raising *con las veinticinco y doscientos cinquenta mil cuentas justicieras y ganaderas* (with the twenty-five and two hundred fifty thousand accounts related to white and black magic). The number 25 in *curandero* symbology is composed of two 12s, each symbolizing the eleven faithful disciples plus Paul, as well as a 1 symbolizing Judas. Twenty-five is then multiplied by ten thousand to increase its power. In this way, Eduardo indirectly invokes the forces of evil associated with 13 to help his work ($12 + 1 = \underline{13} + 12 = 25$), for these are the forces responsible for witchcraft, and therefore most capable of revealing its causes. However, the forces of evil are carefully counterbalanced by the forces of good—the two 12s—in this operation, since $12 + 12 + 1$ also equals 25. This raising thus activates the balanced forces of the *Centro Medio* and, in the process, the evil forces of the *Campo Ganadero*. A *brujo* would raise the *mesa* with *las treinta y trescientos mil cuentas* (symbolizing the thirty pieces of silver Judas received for betraying Christ), which would weigh the invocation toward the

forces of evil. In this phase of the curing session, the two assistants each imbibe one shell of *tabaco* through the nose, but Eduardo abstains.

10. *Tarjo* addressed to all the forces of nature and to the ancients. In this *tarjo* Eduardo invokes the now activated forces of both *campos, justiciero* and *ganadero*—the mountains, lagoons, ancient shrines, streams, gardens of magical plants, and *curanderos*, alive and dead. At its end or in a separate *tarjo,* he then sings all his staffs to life, starting with the Saber of Saint Michael in the *Campo Justiciero* and ending with Satan's Bayonet in the *Campo Ganadero*.

11. Raising of the *San Pedro* remedy. Eduardo pours *tabaco* into a shell, makes a cross with it over the *mesa*, and hands it to one of his assistants, who then bends down beside the can of *San Pedro* brew. The assistant then lifts up his shell alongside the can, makes a cross with it over the remedy, stands, and imbibes the *tabaco* through his nose. This is repeated twice more, once with *agua cananga* by itself and once with Tabu by itself; then this same procedure is performed by the second assistant—who is followed by everyone else present at the session except Eduardo (but only with *tabaco;* not the perfumes). If for some reason a patient cannot get the *tabaco* down his nostrils, he is allowed to swallow it.

12. Purification and presentation of the *San Pedro* remedy and the *curandero* to the *mesa*. One of the assistants brings a full cup of the remedy to Eduardo, who places it on the *mesa* in front of him. He then picks up the *seguro* (herb jar), the dagger, and the cup of *San Pedro*, and he stands up. After serving themselves with one shell of *tabaco* each, his assistants now take positions on both sides of him, and while he performs a *tarjo* in his own name—holding the *seguro*, rattle, dagger, and cup of *San Pedro* at the same time—they simultaneously move their shells along his body from feet to waist, waist to neck, and neck to crown. Next, they imbibe the *tabaco* mixture, and when they have finished, Eduardo performs a *limpia* or cleansing of himself by rubbing the *seguro* all over his body from head to toes. He then sits down, places everything back on the *mesa,* and orally sprays the *seguro* three times with *agua florida*, three times with Tabu and three times with *agua cananga*.

13. The previous step is followed by yet another raising in the name of the remedy, this time performed by Eduardo with one shell of *tabaco*. He then lifts the full cup of *San Pedro* from the *mesa*, drinks it in one draft, massages his head with the empty cup, and blows into the cup three times. Patients and guests are not now also required to raise the

San Pedro brew with *tabaco* like Eduardo, but at this point they too must go through the same procedure of drinking the pure infusion, rubbing, and blowing. To end this phase of the ceremony, Eduardo now serves pure *San Pedro* to his assistants, first presenting their individual servings to the *mesa* and then making a special benediction in the name of each one. Both assistants follow the same procedure in drinking the remedy as did the patients: drinking, rubbing the head, and blowing.

14. Cleansing of all present. Eduardo stands beyond the staffs of the *mesa*, making sure that one of his assistants occupies his seat at the *mesa* at all times, and has the patients and assistants come before him, one a time. As each person comes forth, he rubs him or her from head to foot with the *chungana*, and he then blows on his rattle with a sharp expulsion of air *(sopla)*. When he has done this for everyone else, he performs the procedure on himself. It is now midnight, and this ends the charging of the *mesa*.

The Curing Acts *(Discharing the Mesa)*

1. *Purificación* (purification) of the *mesa*. Eduardo orally sprays his *mesa* with the three perfumes and sugar as he did in the opening ceremony.

2. *Rastreo* (tracking, or tracing). The patient stands beyond the staffs at the front of the *mesa* facing Eduardo, who now sings a *tarjo* in the name of the patient. All present then concentrate on the staffs to see which one vibrates. Once agreement is reached, this staff is given to the patient to hold in his or her left hand over the chest. Everyone now concentrates on the patient and staff, while Eduardo chants a *tarjo* in the name of the staff. This *tarjo* includes all the accounts associated with the staff, and it is intended to activate the patient's spirit, reveal the illness, and invoke the spirits, if any, that are antagonizing the patient. It is followed by a reflective silence that may last five or ten minutes.

3. *Cuenta* (account). As the persons and events of the patient's life begin to be "seen" by Eduardo, he relates them, interspersing his narration with questions and comments. During this phase, other patients or guests may share some of Eduardo's visions. It is now that Eduardo "sees" the causes of *daño* (witchcraft), *enredo* (love magic), or *suerte* (bad luck), if these are the ailments bothering the patient. In serious cases, this is a critical phase in which many effects of the ailment may manifest themselves in the patient.

4. *Desmarco* or *descuenta* (removal or discount). Eduardo sings a final song relating to the accounts of the staff.

5. Raising the patient. During the last song Eduardo's two assistants have taken positions on either side of the patient, and now they "raise" him or her from feet to waist, waist to neck, and neck to the top of the head with one shellful of whatever substance is indicated for the ailment. This procedure is to help remove the cause of the patient's illness by "centering" him or her.

6. Raising the staff. The patient holds the staff over his or her head by its tip and nasally imbibes whatever substance is specified by Eduardo. In severe cases of *daño*, the patient has great difficulty getting the substance down and often vomits (which is considered necessary in the treatment of *daño* induced by food or drink). This can be another critical period in the treatment of serious cases. If the patient cannot get the substance down, one of the assistants or Eduardo himself may have to do so in his or her name, after which Eduardo may still have to perform a symbolic sword battle and the seven somersaults *(siete mortales)* necessary to combat witchcraft.

7. Cleansing of the patient. Once the patient has raised the staff, an assistant takes it from him or her and rubs it all over the patient's body.

8. *Sopla* (blowing) and *chicotea* (violent shake) of the staff. An assistant or Eduardo now sprays the patient's staff three times with whatever liquid is indicated by the account. He then slices the air with the staff in whatever compass direction or directions are indicated, and he returns it to its proper position at the front of the *mesa*.

9. *Salto sobre el fuego* (leap over the fire). After the curing acts are performed for all present, the victims of the witchcraft must then leap four times so that their movements form a cross over a small bonfire of straw lit by Eduardo's assistants. After the jumps, each must then stamp out the fire. Then, as each individual patient steps backwards, an assistant cuts the ground between his or her feet with one of the *mesa* swords. This appears to be a symbolic act indicating "mastery over fire" or "magical heat," a shamanistic attribute that is passed on to the patient in order to purge and purify him or her by exorcising evil spirits. In some cases the *salto* may be performed before the *rastreo* (step 2).

10. *Florecimiento* ("flowering"). For patients whose cures are nearly completed, Eduardo often conducts a final centering ritual. This consists of Eduardo placing the patient within a circle of white corn meal drawn on the ground, his spraying holy water around the patient at the four cardinal points while cutting the spray with a sword, and

then his cutting a final spray in the form of a spiral in front of the patient. After these acts, Eduardo may give the patient some advice or instructions.

11. *Cierre de la cuenta* (closing of the account). This is the same as the opening ceremony. It is performed after Eduardo has repeated steps 1 through 8 for all present except himself, as well as conducted the *florecimiento* and the fire ceremony reserved for victims of witchcraft (step 9).

12. *Refresco* (purification, or "refreshment") of participants and locale. The two assistants orally spray a mixture of holy water, white cornmeal, white flowers, white sugar, sweet-lime juice, and powdered lime in the faces, on the necks (front and back), and over the hands (front and back) of everyone, including Eduardo and each other. While they are "refreshing" the patients, Eduardo gathers up his artifacts in the same order as he put them down at the beginning of the session—*Justiciero, Medio, Ganadero,* and staffs from right to left. All of his artifacts must be put away before sunrise to prevent sunlight from striking them, and any leftover *San Pedro* is buried for the same reason. Once he has packed everything up, he uses his dagger to cut a cross three times in the earth where the *mesa* was laid, and he then sprinkles the *refresco* mixture used by his assistants three times along the cuts in the ground and once in each of the four corners of the *mesa* area, which must not be touched by anyone until noon of the day in progress. All participants are then required to abstain from condiments (especially salt, hot peppers, onions, and garlic), pork, beans, or any plant that grows on a vine or has twisting roots until noon of the day in progress.

Eduardo's mesa

THE MESA ARTIFACTS

This description of Eduardo's mesa is based upon taped discussions he held with Douglas Sharon in the summer of 1970, the fall of 1971, the winter of 1974, and the winter of 1978. From other studies we know that images of saints, archaeological objects, jars of herbs, stones, shells, crystals, staffs, swords, daggers, and rattles all typically appear on northern Peruvian *mesas*. Northern *curanderos* and *brujos*, however, are very individualistic, and each sets up his *mesa* according to his own idiosyncratic needs and inspiration.

Staffs

Campo Ganadero

I.*Bayoneta de Satanás* (Satan's Bayonet): Supposedly from the time of the French Revolution when it was stained with human blood, this artifact symbolizes the malevolent powers of evil, such as Satan, his assistants, and the demons of Hell, as well as certain mountains where these powers are concentrated. *Brujos* conclude midnight pacts with the Devil and petition his aid by applying *canazo* (sugar-cane alcohol, water, and sugar) to this bayonet, followed by the appropriate ceremonies to invoke the thirteen and thirty thousand mystical accounts of Satan. For Eduardo, this sword is symbolically connected to the Triton Shell (1), Snake Stone (2), and Deer Foot (3).

II.*Vara Lechuza* (Owl Staff): This rosewood staff is a symbol of wisdom and vision related to the owl's ability to see in the dark. However, it also symbolizes corpses, cemeteries, the spirits of the dead, and the spirits of pre-Columbian grave objects and ruins. *Brujos* use this staff for purposes of witchcraft, as opposed to *curanderos* who use it for diagnosing and countering the effects of witchcraft. It is symbolically connected to the Owl Stone (13), Vampire Bat Ceramic (14), Bound Corn Stone (28), and the Bound Humans and Whirlpool Stones (29) in the *Campo Ganadero*.

III. *Vara de la Señorita* (Staff of the Single Woman): This staff, made from black *chonta* wood, is symbolic of the sacred highland lagoons and the shawl-wearing female guardian who protects them, along with certain magical plants found near them which are used in healing. *Brujos* use this staff to help a client (whether male or female) to perform *enredo* (entanglement), a love spell on a mate or companion; *curanderos* use it to bring about *desenredo*, disentanglement. In curing, it connects with sweet lime (77) in the *Campo Justiciero*.

Campo (or Centro) Medio

IV. *Vara Serpiente de Moisés y Solomón* (Serpent Staff of Moses and Solomon): This staff of *guayacán* wood is representative of the sun and the oceans, and symbolizes the duality of light and water, as well as all the mountains, lagoons, ancient shrines, streams, and magical herb gardens of northern Peru. Included in the realm of this staff are such personages as Moses, Solomon (the staff symbolizes his collarbone), and Saint Cyprian, all of whom are considered to have been masters of both the magical and religious arts, and therefore capable of harmonizing the two extremes of good and evil, which is the main function of the *Centro Medio* governed by this staff. Working in conjunction with the statue of Saint Cyprian (36), the Serpent Staff is also connected to the Moses and the Red Sea Stone (57) in the *Campo Justiciero.*

Campo Justiciero

V. *Pico de Pez Espada* (Swordfish Beak): This is an authentic swordfish beak symbolizing the seven seas, the powerful fish they contain, and the fish's speed of passage through the water. It is used to locate sailors or fishermen lost at sea, drowned people, shipwrecks, and sunken treasure, or to bring luck to fishermen and sailors. It is one of the artifacts associated with journeys to the underworld, and is connected to the Sea and Winds Stone (33) in the *Centro Medio.*

VI. *Vara Aguila* (Eagle Staff): The Eagle Staff is of black *chonta* wood, with the dried head and claws of an eagle affixed to its top. This staff is under the aegis of the Caesars of Rome, and symbolizes great "vision" (related to the eagle's sharp sight), intelligence, power, ambition, triumph, and good luck, as well as success in love, intellectual pursuits, and business. It is used to bolster morale, to change bad luck, or to guarantee good luck in present and future ventures. It is also a symbol of magical flight, and is connected with sweet lime (77) and to such major mountain peaks as Huascarán, Huandóy, Hualcán, Misti, Pelagato, Monte Aguja, and Machu Picchu.

VII. *Vara del Galgo* (Greyhound Staff): This is a black *chonta* wood staff with an ivory handle in the shape of a greyhound's head. Under the aegis of Saint Jerome, the Greyhound Staff is used when the *curandero* is attempting to locate a lost or stolen object for his petitioner, and because of the Greyhound's tracking ability and sense of smell, this staff is also used to discover the whereabouts of people who have run away. It is additionally a symbol for great speed, and is often referred to as *alcosunca* (a spotted, short-haired dog) or *alcocala* (a hairless dog).

VIII. *Vara Chupaflor* (Hummingbird Staff): This is a rosewood staff used for removing sicknesses or pains by means of the patient's vomiting or sweating, the reference being the hummingbird's capacity to extract plant nectar by sucking. In curing, it connects symbolically with sweet lime (77) and to the "gardens" of magical herbs visited by the shaman in trances.

IX. *Vara de la Virgen de las Mercedes* (Staff of the Virgin of Mercy): This staff is made of black *chonta* wood capped with an expended military cartridge. It symbolizes the seven Churches of early Christianity as well as Moses, Solomon, and all the saints and prayers of the Roman Catholic Church. It is used to promote good luck, especially in intellectual endeavors and marriage, provided those who desire such luck do so for unselfish reasons. The Virgin of Mercy is the patron of the military forces of Peru; thus her staff is a focal point of great force and power on the side of good. It is connected to the Soldier Stone (54), sweet lime (77), Lord of Huamán (70), Saint Paul (61), and Saint Francis (41). The accounts of the Virgin, the Divine Judge, the saints, and Saint Joseph, patron of the home, are all symbolically stored here.

X. *Espada de San Pablo* (Sword of Saint Paul): This sword, supposedly used by a Chilean soldier in the War of the Pacific in the late nineteenth century, symbolizes soldiers, judges, lawyers (especially Saint Paul, the great lawyer of Christianity), and justice in general. It is used to apply divine justice and to make rebellious spirits face reality in the same way as happened to Saul of Tarsus. It connects with the Solider Stone (54).

XI. *Sable de San Miguel Arcángel* (Saber of Saint Michael the Archangel): This is a late-nineteenth-century cavalry officer's sword, and is under the aegis of Saint Michael, chief of the celestial armies of Christianity. As a symbol of Heavenly justice, it is used to purge patients suffering from serious cases of *daño* (witchcraft) and to ward off attacking evil spirits that might appear during a session. It is connected to the Soldier Stone (54) and to Saint Michael's Dagger (47).

XII. *Lata de San Pedro* (can of San Pedro brew): This five-gallon can holds the infusion made from boiling the San Pedro cactus *(Trichocereus pachanoi)*, various herbs, and water for seven hours to extract the juice. The resulting brew is the catalyst for the activation of all the accounts of the *mesa*.

Ground Artifacts

Campo Ganadero

1. *Caracól Triton* (Triton Shell): This shell, discovered in an archeological ruin and connected with Satan's Bayonet (I), is used for love magic. It symbolizes the vulva and the spiral, which is one of the major symbols of the *mesa,* being associated with origins and with the "center." Also called *remolino* (whirlpool), the spiral embodies the first subjective experiences related to San Pedro usage.

2. *Piedra Culebra* (Snake Stone): Found in an archeological ruin, this stone is used to discover the cause of crop damage or to aid in the growth of crops. Connected to Satan's Bayonet (I) and to the Wheat Stone (26), it is also called *colambo* and *macanche,* other terms for snakes used in contemporary Moche folklore. *Colambos,* for example, are trained snakes believed to protect small farms.

3. *Pata de Venado* (Deer Foot): This right front foot of a deer is used to detect invading spirits and to exorcise spirts in cases of possession. It symbolizes the swiftness and elusiveness of spiritual flight, and is connected to Satan's Bayonet (I).

4. *Botella de aguardiente* (bottle of cane alcohol) (missing): This is one of the ingredients used in the preparation of *tabaco* (see 52) and is also used as a libation to any spirits that may be attracted to a séance. It is associated with the intoxicating powers of the Devil, who must be resisted when *tabaco* is imbibed through the nostrils.

5. *Pedernales* (flints): These three colored flints (one black, one white, and one purple) are fire symbols used for making sparks to chase off attacking evil spirts. They balance the functions of the three crystals (73) in the *Campo Justiciero.*

6. *Cerámica Mono* (Monkey Ceramic): This fragment of pre-Columbian pottery found at Chan Chan depicts a monkey and symbolizes its tricks. It is used to invoke jungle animals in order to play pranks, to confuse a person with whom one may be annoyed, or to oppose such actions by another.

7. *Piedra Cuy Negro* (Black Guinea Pig Stone): Found in an archeological ruin, this stone is used for diagnostic practices alone or with a live guinea pig (when performing entrail divination). It symbolizes witchcraft.

8. *Piedra Loro Negro* (Black Parrot Stone): Found in an archeological ruin, this stone is used to discover whether damage to crops was caused by a *brujo.* It also symbolizes a black crow *(cuervo negro).*

9. *Piedra Ojo* (Eye Stone): This eye-shaped fragment of a meteor found in an archeological ruin is used to cure *daño* affecting human eyes. Once activated by the *curandero,* it manifests positively as an "eye of heaven."

10. *Piedra Corazón* (Heart Stone): Supposedly found in the mouth of a dead man from an ancient tomb near Moche, this heart-shaped stone is used to cure *daño* directed against the human heart.

11. *Piedra Riñon* (Kidney Stone): This stone from an archeological ruin is used to cure *daño* focused on the human kidneys.

12. *Piedra Pene* (Phallus Stone): This stone, found in an ancient tomb, is used to heal the male sex organ when it is afflicted by *daño.*

13. *Piedra Lechuza* (Owl Stone): Shaped like an owl, this stone from the archeological ruins of Huaca Prieta is used to invoke the spirits of pre-Columbian peoples in order to break spells cast by sorcerers. It is connected to the Owl Staff (II).

14. *Cerámica Murciélago Vampiro* (Vampire Bat Ceramic): Found in the archeological ruins of Huaca del Sol (Sun Temple) near Moche, this fragment of pre-Columbian pottery depicts a vampire bat. It is used to enter ancient ruins in order to invoke the malicious spirits of the dead dwelling there and to detect the cause of witchcraft. This artifact is connected with the Owl Stone (13) and the Owl Staff (II).

15. *Piedra Laguna de Huaca Prieta* (Lagoon Stone from Huaca Prieta): Shaped like a highland lagoon, this stone was found at Huaca Prieta, a ruin often invoked by sorcerers. It is a water symbol used to call such powers and "charms" of the ancients as a green toad *(sapo verde)* or ducks *(patos).*

16. *Cerámica Zorro* (Fox Ceramic): This fragment of pre-Columbian pottery depicts a fox, which Eduardo associates with the moon. It was found in the ruins of Chan Chan, and is used to trick one's enemies. In addition to symbolizing the ability to overcome setbacks and obstacles with the astuteness of a fox, it also symbolizes misfortune and danger caused by guile and deception.

17. *Piedra Rosa Candela* (Rose Fire-Stone): This red and black stone from Huaca Prieta is used to invoke the aid of the spirits of archeological ruins in undoing *daño* performed by fire.

18. *Piedra Ojos Dobles y Remolino* (Double-Eyed Whirlpool Stone): Associated with negative herbs, this stone from an archeological ruin is used to undo *daño* to eyesight and to invoke the spirits of the ancients. It also symbolizes a spiral.

19. *Piedra Rodilla o Macana* (Knee or Club Stone): This knee-shaped stone is used to counter *daño*. Found in an archeological ruin, it also symbolizes a club *(macana)* or the blows *(golpes)* associated with *daño*.

20. *Pito para las huacas* (whistle for ancient shrines): This ancient ceramic ocarina from a tomb is used to invoke the spirits of the dead and of the pre-Columbian past. The spirit of the actual person with whom it was buried is believed to be captured inside it.

21. *Puros* (cigars): Cigar smoke is used both to purify the *mesa* and to overcome those sorcerer's spells effected with smoke. To achieve either purpose, Eduardo performs an operation called *fumada,* which involves rapidly puffing on a cigar or cigarette until it is used up.

22. *Piedra de la Señorita* (Stone of the Single Woman): This stone, from the vicinity of the highland town of Santiago de Chuco, symbolizes a nearby lagoon and lagoons in general, as well as the female guardian of these power loci. It is utilized with the Ancient Single Woman Ceramic (23) and the Staff of the Single Woman (III) in undoing love magic.

23. *Cerámica Señorita Gentila* (Ancient Single Woman Ceramic): This piece of pre-Columbian pottery found at Chan Chan is utilized with the Stone of the Single Woman (22) to overcome love magic. The ancient single woman is conceptualized as a shawl-wearing herbalist, guardian of the sacred lagoons and plants, who carries a bouquet of flowers in her hand symbolizing all the magical flora.

24. *Piedra Taco de Zapato de Mujer* (Stone of the Heel of a Woman's Shoe): This stone, shaped like its name, was found at Huaca Prieta. It is used to bring back women who are lost or who have run away.

25. *Piedra Paratón-Siete Suertes* (Elevated Seven Fortunes Stone): This stone, found on Cerro Paratón-Siete Suertes, a mountain located near the town of Pimentel, is used to aid victims of *daño,* particularly when it affects business.

26. *Piedra Trigo* (Wheat Stone): This wheat-shaped stone, from an archeological ruin, is used to discover the cause of damage to crops or to promote their fertility. It connects with Snake Stone (2).

27. *Cerámica Pie Derecho de Hombre* (Right Foot of a Man Ceramic)-: This is a piece from a pre-Columbian pot discovered at the ruins of Chan Chan. Depicting a man's right foot, it is used to locate men who are lost or who have run away, as well as to discover theft. It is connected to Saint Cyprian (36) in the *Centro Medio.*

28. *Piedra Maíz Atado* (Bound Corn Stone): Shaped like two shocks of corn tied together, this stone is used for undoing love magic. It is from an archeological ruin, and is connected to the Owl Staff (II).

29. *Piedras Humanos Atados y Remolino* (Bound Humans and Whirlpool Stones): These stones found at Huaca del Sol depict a bound male and female, and are used for undoing love magic. They also symbolize a spiral, and are connected to the Owl Staff (II).

30. *Concha* (shell): Associated with the Bound Humans Stone (29) and with love spells, this vulva-shaped shell is used for the *rastreo* (tracing) of women patients in order to determine their character.

Centro Medio

31 *El Sol* (The Sun): This is a bronze sunburst symbolizing the sun as it climbs into the morning sky from 6:00 A.M. until noon. It is the fire symbol par excellence.

32. *Bola de bronce* (bronze disk): This disk represents the sun complete with corona, and is identified with the light and the 24-hour day.

33. *Piedra del Mar y los Vientos* (Sea and Winds Stone): This stone, found in an ancient tomb near the ocean, is used to "see" drowned people, shipwrecks, and articles that have been lost at sea or on the beach. Like the Swordfish Beak (V) in the *Campo Justiciero* with which it is connected, it symbolizes the seven seas.

34. *Seguro del curandero* (healer's glass herb jar): This is the artifact in which Eduardo's power is most concentrated. It is his main talisman, his alter ego, and he uses it for defense, divination, diagnosis, and treatment. In addition to certain standard ingredients (such as saints' medals, gold and silver coins, perfume, sugar candy, lime juice, and hair from the crown of Eduardo's head, it also contains an assortment of magical herbs selected according to Eduardo's personal preferences. Seven accounts are stored in it under the direction of Saint Jerome, tamer of wild animals, while Saint Anthony, who helps to find lost objects, is also here, along with the Peruvian Saint Martin, a miraculous healer (see 53), and the wise magician-king Solomon. The *seguro* (which literally means "protection") is also called *pomo* (glass jar) and *ajuste* (covenant).

35. *Piedra Laguna Shimbe* (Shimbe Lagoon Stone): Taken by Eduardo from the bottom of the Shimbe Lagoon during his first ritual bath in August 1970, this stone symbolizes the lagoon as well as his *maestro* don Florentino García, whose spirit Eduardo summons for assistance during a séance.

36. *San Cipriano* (Saint Cyprian): According to Christian folklore, Cyprian was a magician and sorcerer who was converted to Christianity and became a martyr. He is the patron saint of many folk healers from northern Peru, and is the mediator between the *Campo Ganadero* and *Campo Justiciero,* since he is of these two realms himself. Cyprian is also the saint best suited to strike a bargain with Satan in order to cure witchcraft, or to aid the *curandero* on a journey to the Underworld. Eduardo's statue is made of *sapote* wood and sits on a deck of Spanish divining cards with a red bag of divinatory runes at its feet, symbolizing the ambiguity of both fate and fortune.

37. *Piedras Minerales y Caudales* (Mineral and Fortune Stones): These two stones from archeological ruins are used to bring wealth and good fortune. *Minerales* represent not only the mountains from which mineral wealth is extracted, but also a sleeping lion, called a *carbunco* in local folklore, which protects the second stone, symbolic of a treasure chest and implying the fortunes *(caudales)* obtained from these mountains.

38. *Espejo de cristál* (crystal "mirror"): This clear rock crystal from Rio Seco is supposed to reflect events at a distance related to and explaining cases of daño. A cat fetish (not in this photograph) normally sits on it for defensive purposes; the sharp "vision," swiftness, and ferocity of the feline being used to discover and counter attacks by *brujos.* The twenty-five balanced accounts of the *Centro Medio* are stored in this mirror, which is also considered to be a pyramid.

39. *Paño de gentil* (cloth from an ancient tomb): This cotton cloth is used to wrap Saint Cyprian when the *mesa* artifacts are stored. During a ceremony, it is kept under the white linen cloth (78), on top of which the artifacts are placed.

Campo Justiciero

40. *Seguro de paciente* (patient's herb jar): This is a glass bottle containing images of saints in plastic, gold and silver coins from the nineteenth century, three types of perfumes, white sugar, sweet lime juice, hair from the crown of the patient's head, and a large variety of magical herbs from the Andean highlands. It belongs to a patient who asked Eduardo to place it at the head of his *mesa* during sessions in order to purify and "charge" it, so as to bring good fortune in the petitioner's business.

41. *San Francisco de Asís* (Saint Francis of Assisi): Eduardo modeled and fired his own ceramic statue of this, his favorite saint. Friend of wildlife, especially birds, Saint Francis is a symbol of divine strength

and goodness, and is especially powerful in exorcising evil spirits in conjunction with the Virgin of Mercy Staff (IX).

42. *Niño Jesus de Praga* (Child Jesus of Prague): This statue, carved in wood from a *sapote* tree, carries the world in its hand as if it were a toy. The world is also symbolized by the rattle (59), with which the child Jesus statue is ritually connected.

43. *Virgen del Carmen* (Virgin of Carmen): This statue of the Virgin Mary as she appeared at Carmen, Mexico is carved in wood from the *sapote* tree. Mary is the overseer of Purgatory, and along with Saint Cyprian mediates journeys to the Underworld.

44. *Piedra María Magdalena* (Mary Magdalene Stone) (under rope): This stone from an archeological ruin is placed near the crucifix (51) at the feet of Christ. Mary Magdalene, converted from a life of sin as was Saint Cyprian, channels the power of evil constructively.

45. *Piedra Pecho de la Virgen* (Virgin's Breast Stone): Found in an archeological ruin, this stone is used in petitions of mercy and for curing pains and burns.

46. *Perla* ("Pearl" Shell): This is a flat bivalve shell used in imbibing *tabaco* through the nostrils. Since it is on the left side of the *Campo Justiciero,* it is used by the *alzador* ("raiser" or assistant) to the *curandero*'s left, and it is somewhat associated with the *Campo Ganadero.*

47. *Puñal de San Miguel Arcángel* (Dagger of Saint Michael the Archangel): This dagger is used in Eduardo's defense to protect himself against spirit attacks from the *Campo Ganadero.* During the entire curing ceremony he holds it in his left hand, and it connects symbolically with the Saber of Saint Michael (XI), which is also effective against evil spirits.

48. *San Antonio* (Saint Anthony): Carved from *sapote* wood, this statue is used to discover lost or stolen objects.

49. *Virgen de la Purísima Concepción* (Virgin of the Immaculate Conception): This statue was carved by Eduardo from a *palo de sangre* stick brought to him by a friend who had it "baptized" by a healer at the Huaringa lagoons. It is used against *daño* involving hemorrhages, and it also symbolizes spiritual birth.

50. *Concha Fuente de la Virgen* (Fountain of the Virgin Shell): Found in an archeological ruin, this large oyster shell supposedly has a shape reminiscent of the Virgin Mary. Symbolizing a return from death (rebirth), it serves to hold a potent infusion of San Pedro and several purgative herbs used in cases of *daño* induced by the mouth (i.e., poisoning).

51. *Cristo y el Calvário* (Crucified Christ): This crucifix of *pial* wood is the "center" of the *mesa* from which Eduardo draws his strength. It is placed on top of a prayer book of the Franciscan Tertiary Order (a lay order), which thus functions as its altar. The crucifix is the axis of the entire *mesa*, and the accounts relating to the seven miracles, or "justices," of Christ are stored here, as are the twelve thousand accounts of the *Campo Justiciero*.

52. *Vasija para tabaco* (bowl for tobacco mixture): *Tabaco* contains the following ingredients: dried black unprocessed leaf tobacco (79); three perfumes—*agua cananga* (74), *agua florida* (75), and Tabu (76); sweet lime juice (77); cane alcohol (4); white sugar (66); and boiled San Pedro (XII). *Tabaco* is "raised" (imbibed through the nostrils) by the *curandero*, his two assistants, and all patients and observers at certain intervals during a session. It is the auxiliary catalyst of a séance.

53. *Perla* ("Pearl Shell): This is a flat, bivalve shell used for imbibing the portions of *tabaco* served to patients undergoing therapy and to the *alzador* on the curer's right. It forms a set with the small shell to its left which is used to measure and serve the *tabaco* for "raising."

54. *Piedra Militar* (Soldier Stone): Found in an archeological ruin near Cerro Paruque in the highlands, this stone works with the statue (61) and sword (X) of Saint Paul in applying divine justice. It forms a power nexus with the last three staffs of the *Campo Justiciero:* Virgin of Mercy (IX), Saint Paul (X), and Saint Michael (XI).

55. *San Martín de Porres* (Saint Martin of Porres): Saint Martin was a Peruvian mulatto famous for his work among the poor and the sick. He is considered to be a great healer, and carries a broom because during his lifetime he cheerfully performed menial chores. With this broom he is believed to sweep or cleanse the patient's soul.

56. *Concha San Juan Bautista* (Saint John the Baptist's Shell): This large oyster shell, brought from the ocean, is used for sprinkling holy water and for baptisms. It symbolizes rebirth by means of a holy sacrament.

57. *Piedra Moisés y el Mar Rojo* (Moses and the Red Sea Stone): This stone from an archeological ruin is used to keep away evil spirits. It symbolizes miraculous passage, that is, rebirth, and is connected to the Serpent Staff of Moses (IV) in the *Centro Medio* as well as to the Staff of the Virgin of Mercy (IX) in the *Campo Justiciero*.

58. *Piedra Nacimiento de Jesus* (Birth of Jesus Stone): This stone is for protection against invading spirits. It is also a symbol of spiritual birth.

59. *Chungana* (gourd rattle): This wooden-handled gourd rattle contain-

ing dried *huarango* seeds activates all the *mesa* accounts. In conjunction with the *tarjos* (chants) of the *curandero* and reinforced by sweet odors (perfumes), sweet tastes (sugar), and the relaxed state caused by San Pedro, it is supposed to render all spirits (the patient's and those causing *daño*) susceptible to therapy. The rattle symbolizes the human skull and the earth on its axis, as well as being another manifestation of the spiral. It works in conjunction with the world carried by the Christ Child (42), and defensive functions against evil spirits are also attributed to it. It is incised with the following: the Star of David, symbols for the three angels of light, the symbol of Christ and the Sacred Host, a spiral, the sun, and the moon.

60. *Soga de hábito de monje* (rope from a monk's habit): From a monastery in Lima, this gift from a grateful patient is worn around Eduardo's neck throughout the séance to support the defensive functions of his dagger and rattle. By swinging it over his head, he can scourge and drive off evil spirits.

61. *San Pablo* (Saint Paul): This statue, carved from the wood of the *sapote* tree, is symbolic of divine justice, for Paul was a lawyer. It connects with the Virgin of Mercy Staff (IX) and the Sword of Saint Paul (X), which, together with the Saber of Saint Michael (XI), are instrumental in removing Judas from Satan's realm (the *Campo Ganadero*) during the raising of the twenty-five thousand accounts of the *Centro Medio.*

62. *Piedra de la cueva del Cerro Chalpón* (stone from the cave of Chalpón Mountain): This fire symbol, believed to have great curative powers, is from the cave of a Christian ascetic, Father Guatemala, who is believed to have ascended to Heaven. To this day, people from all over Peru make pilgrimages to his holy shrine near the town of Motupe. Chalpón is volcanic; thus this stone additionally symbolizes an erupting volcano, and it is also symbolic of eternal rebirth after an initiatory return to the earth-womb.

63. *Cristál Jacob* (Jacob's Crystal): This crystal, which is used as a defense against sorcerers' attacks, symbolizes rapid, clear "vision" resulting from regeneration.

64. *Cristál Ojo de Culebra* (Snake-Eye Crystal): This crystal represents animate and inanimate defenses coming from nature, as well as rapid, clear "vision" resulting from regeneration.

65. *Perla* ("Pearl" Shell): This is a flat, bivalve seashell used by Eduardo for imbibing *tabaco* through the nostrils. Each of the five pearl-bearing shells (46, 50, 53, 56, 65) symbolizes the human hand, the moon, the sea (considered to be a great mirror), and spiritual rebirth.

66. *Azúcar blanco* (white sugar): This is a package of granulated white sugar used in the *tabaco* mixture, the *seguros,* and the purification ceremonies for the *mesa.* Like Tabu (75), it symbolizes sweetness and receptivity to therapy. Sometimes it is supplemented by hard sugar candy.

67. *Caracól en Rollo* (Roll "Snail" Shell): Found in the archeological ruins of Chan Chan, this shell is used to undo love magic. It is another spiral symbol, this time with a phallic shape.

68. *Vasija para refresco* (bowl for "refreshment" or purification): This bowl is used to hold a mixture of holy water, white cornmeal, and lime, which "refreshes" and purifies both the *mesa* and the patients after the session is over.

69. *El Señor de Huamán* (Lord of Huamán): This limestone statue of Christ as Divine Judge sitting on a throne in Heaven after His ascension is a symbol of justice and humility. It is used in petitions, to win friends, and to lend general assistance when needed. It is connected with the Virgin of Mercy Staff (IX).

70. *Taza* (cup): This cup is used for serving San Pedro by itself at midnight. Normally it occupies the position held by white sugar (66), but it was moved to make room for the three perfumes (75, 76, 77), which were laid on their sides for better display in the photograph.

71. *Cristál Arca de Noé* (Noah's Ark Crystal): This crystal representing Noah's ark symbolizes a new beginning for human and animal life after emergence from the primal waters.

72. *Cristales Rayos Blancos* (White Ray Crystals): These three white quartz crystals are fire symbols used for defense. Found near the ancient Huaca del Sol, one represents a bullet, another a car, and the third a single die. Together they symbolize the speed and good fortune associated with magical flight.

73. *Agua cananga* (red perfume): This is a perfume used in the *seguros* which is also used to purify the *mesa* and occasionally for a patient to imbibe through the nostrils. It symbolizes purifying fire.

74. *Agua florida* (scented water): This perfume is used like *agua cananga,* and in special cases a patient will imbibe it through the nostrils without its being mixed with other ingredients. It symbolizes sacred herb "gardens" and flowers.

75. *Tabu* (Tabu cologne): Used like *agua cananga* and *agua florida,* this cologne is also employed in the *curandero*'s petition to God during the séance. It symbolizes sweetness and receptivity to therapy.

76. *Lima dulce* (sweet lime): Used like the three perfumes, sweet lime is connected with the Single Woman Staff (III), the Eagle Staff (VI), the Hummingbird Staff (VIII) and the Virgin of Mercy Staff (IX).

77. *Mantél blanco de lino* (white linen cloth): This is the cloth on which the artifacts of the *mesa* are placed.

78. *Tabaco negro* (black tobacco): This is the principal ingredient in *tabaco*, and is referred to by Eduardo either with the Quechua word for tobacco, *sayri*, or as *huaman tabaco* (falcon tobacco). The latter designation refers to the sharp sight of the falcon, since *tabaco* is believed to clear the mind and to stimulate great vision in divining and in perceiving the attacks of sorcerers. Together with San Pedro, tobacco is supposed to activate a sixth sense within the individual.

REFERENCES

Foster, George M. and Barbara Anderson
    1978   *Medical Anthropology*. New York:John Wiley and Sons.

Furst, Peter T.
    1976   *Hallucinogens and Culture*. San Francisco: Chandler &
            Sharp Publishers, Inc.

Harwood, Alan
    1977   *Rx: Spiritist as Needed: A Study of a Puerto Rican Com-
            munity Mental Health Resource*. New York: John Wiley
            and Sons.

Kennedy, John G.
    1974   Cultural Psychiatry. In: *Handbook of Social and Cultural
            Anthropology*. John J. Honigman, ed. New York: Rand
            McNally College Publishing Company.

Kiev, Ari
    1972   *Transcultural Psychiatry*. New York: Free Press.

Lambo, Thomas A.
    1964   Patterns of Psychiatric Care in Developing African Coun-
            tries. In: *Magic, Faith, and Healing: Studies in Primitive
            Psychiatry Today*. Ari Kiev, ed., pp. 443-53. New York:
            Free Press.

Point International, To The
    1978   Witchdoctors Accepted as Professionals. 5:21:30, May 26.

Ruiz, Pedro, and John Langrod
    1976a   Psychiatry and Folk Healing: A Dichotomy? *American
            Journal of Psychiatry* 133:1:95-6.
    1976b   Psychiatrists and Spiritual Healers: Partners in Commu-
            nity Mental Health. In: *Anthropology and Mental Health:
            Setting a New Course*. Joseph Westermeyer, ed., pp. 77-81.
            The Hague: Mouton Publishers.
    1976c   The Role of Folk Healers in Community Mental Health
            Services. *Community Mental Health Journal* 12:4:392-8.
    1977   The Ancient Art of Folk Healing: African Influence in a
            New York Community Mental Health Center. In: *Tradi-
            tional Healing: New Science or New Colonialism?* Philip
            Singer, ed. New York: Conch Magazine Limited.

Seguin, Carlos A.
1970   Psiquiatría Folklórica. In: *Psiquiatría* Peruana. Oscar
        Valdivia and Alberto Péndola, eds., 1:301-39. Lima: Amauta.
1974   Introducción a la Psiquiatría Folklórica. *Acta Psiquía-
        trica y Psicológica de América Latina.* 20:305-42.
1977   Estado Actual y Perspectivas de la Psiquiatría Folklór-
        ica. In: *Psiquiatría* Peruana. Saul Peña, *Oscar Valdivia,
        José Alva, eds., 4:100-105. Lima: Talleres Gráficos P.L.* Vil-
        lanueva S.A.

Sharon, Douglas
1978   *Wizard of the Four Winds: A Shaman's Story.* New York:
        Free Press.

Singer, Philip, ed.
1977   *Traditional Healing: New Science or New Colonialism?*
        New York: Conch Magazine, Ltd.

Torrey, E. Fuller
1972   *The Mind Game: Witchdoctors and Psychiatrists.* New
        York: Emerson Hall Publishers.

Velimirovic, Boris, ed.
1978   *Modern Medicine and Medical Anthropology in the United
        States-Mexico Border Population.* Washington, D.C.:
        PAHO Scientific Publication No. 359.

World Health Organization
1978   *The Promotion and Development of Traditional Medicine.*
        Geneva: WHO Technical Report Series No. 622.